Why Should I
Believe the
BIBLE?

Why Should I
Believe the
BIBLE?

An Easy-to-Understand Guide to Scripture's Trustworthiness

BARBOUR
PUBLISHING

Print ISBN 978-1-62029-910-4

eBook Editions:
Adobe Digital Edition (.epub) 978-1-62416-334-0
Kindle and MobiPocket Edition (.prc) 978-1-62416-333-3

Published by Barbour Publishing, Inc., P.O. Box 719, Uhrichsville, Ohio 44683, www.barbourbooks.com

Our mission is to publish and distribute inspirational products offering exceptional value and biblical encouragement to the masses.

Member of the
Evangelical Christian
Publishers Association

Printed in the United States of America.

Contents

Introduction

This book is designed to give you confidence in your Bible.

God gave us His Word to direct us to Him, to tell us how to live this life, and to explain the future glories of eternity in His presence. But there are times when the massiveness, complexity, antiquity—and yes, mystery—of the Bible can confuse and even overwhelm us. *Why Should I Believe the Bible?* will provide the understanding and clarity you need to truly "get" God's Word.

The first portion of this book, *Answers to Your Bible Questions,* explains why the Bible really does make sense. . . that we can know where it actually came from. . .that we have evidence to support its claims of truth. For seventy-five tough questions—the kind raised by both skeptics and honest believers—you'll find clear, intellectually and spiritually satisfying answers.

The second section of this book, *Understand Your Bible,* shows you how the historical, geographic, literary, and other contexts of scripture can clarify what you read and study. Designed to remove the obstacles to understanding scripture, it will give you solutions to the roadblocks that keep many people from regularly reading and truly grasping God's Word.

Finally, this book provides a plan for reading through the Bible in a year. Once you've had your barriers removed and your questions answered, why not begin a personal journey through the fascinating world of scripture?

We wish you all the best in your study.

THE EDITORS

Answers

to Your
B I B L E
Questions

75 Reasons to Believe Scripture's
Truth and Trustworthiness

ED STRAUSS

Contents

1

Does the Bible as it was originally recorded contain any mistakes? Are our copies still completely error-free today?

In answer to the first question: No, the Word of God, as originally given, contains no mistakes. Paul tells us, "All Scripture is given by inspiration of God" (2 Timothy 3:16 NKJV), and God doesn't make mistakes. However, Bible scholars recognize that as the scriptures were hand-copied over the centuries, minor scribal errors crept into the text. The Bible as we have it today, therefore, is not completely free of *human* error. This is what evangelical Christians mean when they say the Bible is "inerrant in its original autographs."

While the Hebrew scribes took great care to copy the scriptures accurately, they occasionally made mistakes. This was understandable, given that the Hebrew text had no separations between words and that the words consisted of only consonants—no vowels.

During the AD 600s to 900s, Jewish scribes called Masoretes followed very strict rules for making copies of the text and added helpful vowel points to the consonants. This reduced scribal errors dramatically. The Masoretic Text (MT) was so renowned for being error-free that it was accepted as the official version of the Old Testament.

But what about inaccuracies introduced into the text *before* the Masoretes? Until 1947, skeptics argued that there were probably so many mistakes in the Hebrew text that there was no way of telling *how* closely the MT resembled the original documents.

That year, however, a remarkable discovery was made. Jars full of ancient scrolls were discovered in caves near the Dead Sea in Israel. These scrolls dated back two thousand years to between 225 BC–AD 70. The jars contained at least fragments of every Old Testament book but Esther. The "Dead Sea Scrolls," as they came to be known, have confirmed the remarkable accuracy of the Masoretic Text. Yes, there are differences between the MT and certain manuscripts, but the MT is virtually identical to a majority of the ancient copies.

2
What kinds of errors did the scribes make as they copied the text?

The books of 1 and 2 Kings and their "companion" books, 1 and 2 Chronicles, include an example of what is clearly a copyist's error.

First and 2 Kings, which scholars generally agree were compiled between 562–538 BC, detail the history of the kingdoms of Israel and Judah. The parallel histories recorded in 1 and 2 Chronicles focus on Judah, and scholars date them to Ezra's day, some one hundred years later. When recounting the same historical events, Chronicles usually differs from Kings only in that it supplies extra information about the kingdom of Judah.

But here's one striking discrepancy:

The writer of Kings writes, "Jehoiachin was eighteen years old when he became king, and he reigned in Jerusalem three months" (2 Kings 24:8 NKJV). However, Chronicles states: "Jehoiachin was eight years old when he became king, and he reigned in Jerusalem three months and ten days" (2 Chronicles 36:9 NKJV). The ten days is accounted for by the fact that the compiler of Chronicles is, as usual, supplying extra details. The real question is this: Was Jehoiachin eighteen or eight when he became king?

Second Kings 24:15 tells us that Jehoiachin was married at the time he became king and had more than one wife, so obviously he was eighteen, not eight. Indeed, one ancient Hebrew manuscript differs from the Masoretic Text and has "eighteen" in *both* 2 Chronicles 36:9 and 2 Kings 24:8.

So how did this error happen? Well, the Hebrew text of 2 Kings 24:8 literally reads "*son of eight ten years Jehoiachin,*" and the text for 2 Chronicles 36:9 would have originally said the same thing. Very likely, a later scribe, while copying the passage in 2 Chronicles, lost his place and his eyes skipped over the word *ten* to the next word, "years."

3

Wasn't the book of Genesis passed down as oral traditions for hundreds of years?

Skeptics have insisted that the accounts of Abraham, Isaac, and Jacob existed for hundreds of years after their day as oral traditions. That, they say, is because writing was not prevalent at that time in human history. Therefore, the argument goes, the stories—because they were passed down by word of mouth—were corrupted to such an extent that they have little or no actual historical value.

However, Genesis 11:27–28 says that Abraham (around 2166–1991 BC) emigrated from Ur in Chaldea, where writing (even schools) existed. Abraham was a shepherd by choice, but he was not an illiterate nomad. On the contrary, he was a wealthy and, very probably, literate man. In addition, thousands of clay tablets containing writing in a phonetic Semitic version of cuneiform (a writing system used in ancient times) have been discovered at the ancient city of Ebla, just two hundred miles north of Canaan. Many of these writings date to 2500 BC, hundreds of years before Abraham's birth.

In addition, the book of Genesis gives indications of being written in stages, as each succeeding generation, in their old age, added its own story to the ongoing narrative. One example of this is found in Genesis 35:27–29, which describes Jacob returning to his father in Hebron and Isaac's death a few years after. The story of Jacob's adventures in Haran was likely written then. Just *before* Isaac died, however, Jacob's son Joseph had been presumed dead. But after Jacob learned that Joseph was still alive, their combined story continues (in the period *before* Isaac's death), beginning with the statement, "This is the history of Jacob" (Genesis 37:2 NKJV).

Moreover, the cultural elements mentioned in Genesis, from traditions to laws to styles of covenants, all bear the earmarks of authenticity for the time and area in which they were said to have happened. In other words, they are accurate historical accounts.

4
How does the excavation of ancient Ebla shed light on the Bible?

In 1974–75, Italian archaeologist Paolo Matthiae was excavating the mound of Tell Mardikh in Syria when his team discovered a room containing nearly eighteen hundred clay tablets. The tablets dated from around 2500 BC to 2250 BC, the date the city was destroyed. It turns out Matthiae had unearthed the records for Ebla, an ancient city and trade empire that flourished and was sacked nearly ten centuries before Moses.

The writing on many of the tablets was in a hitherto unknown language, but as Dr. Pettinato (the team's epigrapher) deciphered them, he discovered that Ebla had a complex code of laws, many of which resembled the Old

Testament commandments, which would be written about a thousand years later. Sacrifices for sin, purification rites, and even scapegoats were known in Ebla. This contradicted skeptics who had previously argued that Moses couldn't have written his law at the time of the Exodus "because codified laws didn't exist that early."

The Ebla tablets also contain many Semitic names, such as Adam, Abraham, Esau, Ishmael, David, and Saul. They also discuss the Canaanites and the Hittites and refer to ancient Urusalima (Jerusalem), Hazor, Megiddo, and other cities mentioned in the Bible.

Dr. Pettinato reported that Sodom and Gomorrah were named as cities with which Ebla traded. Other scholars dispute this, claiming that the inscriptions instead stand for the names of cities in Syria.

Much of the early speculation that the tablets contained the name of *Yah* (short for *Yahweh*) as endings of people's names is now also disputed. Nevertheless, the discovery of the ancient library of Ebla has done much to confirm many of the Bible's accounts and to shed light on the ancient civilizations that were the backdrop of the Old Testament.

5
Did ancient patriarchs like Methuselah actually live hundreds of years?

Until just a few years ago, many people responded with incredulity when they read the biblical accounts of the ancient patriarchs living for centuries. (Some still do.) For example, according to the scriptures, Methuselah died when he was 969 years old (Genesis 5:27).

In recent years, however, microbiologists and molecular geneticists have learned that aging is largely caused by accumulative damage to our DNA, the hereditary material found in nearly every cell in the human body. Scientists are also exploring molecular repair and rejuvenation of deteriorated cells and tissues to extend the human lifespan. They're confident that they'll eventually be able to stop the aging process so that humans will live hundreds or even thousands of years.

Suddenly, biblical patriarchs living for several centuries doesn't seem so incredible.

Many Christians believe that before the Flood (Genesis 6–8), mankind's DNA wasn't as easily damaged or susceptible to aging as it is today. In addition, the earth's magnetic field was stronger and a layer of water (in the form of ice crystals) shielded it from most ultraviolet radiation. But after the Flood, the shielding was gone, damage to the DNA began to accumulate, and lifespans began to shorten. Shem lived 600 years, Arphaxad 438 years, Peleg 239 years, Terah 205 years, Abraham 175 years, Jacob 147 years, and

Joseph 110 years (see Genesis 11:10–26, 32; 25:7; 47:28; 50:26).

Some Christians, however, believe that these great ages are not to be taken literally, but that they merely echo Babylonian myths that included accounts of ancients living many centuries. They point out that the 110 years Joseph is said to have lived was considered the "ideal age" in Egyptian society. They believe, therefore, that these numbers are symbolic.

Nevertheless, the ages of Abraham and Isaac and Jacob are so embedded in the details of their stories, and make such precise sense mathematically, that it's difficult to believe they're merely symbolic.

6

How do the patriarchs' ages make such precise sense mathematically?

If you compare dates within the lives of Isaac, Ishmael, Jacob, and Joseph (scattered throughout the book of Genesis), you'll see that these so-called random dates are perfectly synchronized.

Let's have a look: the Bible tells us that Isaac was sixty years old when Jacob was born (Genesis 25:26). Now, Isaac died at 180, so Jacob was 120 when his father passed away (Genesis 35:28–29). This was ten years before Jacob entered Egypt at age 130 (Genesis 47:9). This was also the second year of the famine, so Joseph was thirty-nine, since 30 + 7 good years + 2 bad years = 39 total years (Genesis 41:46, 53; 45:6).

Now, 130 – 39 = 91, so Jacob was 91 years old when Joseph was born at the end of Jacob's fourteen-year work contract with Laban (Genesis 30:25; 31:41). Since 91 – 14 = 77, Jacob was 77 (and Isaac, therefore, 137) when Isaac thought he was dying and blessed Jacob, who then fled to Haran.

Isaac believed he was about to die when he was 137, but he needn't have worried. After all, he lived another forty-three years and died at the ripe old age of 180 (Genesis 35:28). So why did he believe he was doomed to die at that age? He was fatalistic. Isaac's older brother, Ishmael, had died at exactly the age of 137 (Genesis 25:17), and Isaac thought *he'd* also die at that age.

Either the author of Genesis carefully worked out how all

these scattered dates intricately interlocked before he began to write, or (more likely) these are the *actual* dates that work out with such precision because they are real.

This then means that Isaac actually lived 180 years, Ishmael lived 137 years, Jacob lived 147 years, and Joseph lived 110 years—even though most of these ages are well beyond the maximum lifespan today.

7
Why does the Bible say that Philistines lived in Canaan in Abraham's day?

In 1175 BC, during the reign of Ramesses III, a massive migration of people from Greece, Crete, and Anatolia launched an attack on Egypt. These invaders, whom historians call Sea Peoples, attacked Egypt by sea and by land. After being repulsed, however, they retreated and settled along the coast of Canaan. Chief among them were the Peleset (P'listi), which is why all these people groups were collectively known as *Philistines*.

However, according to the Bible, Philistines were *already* living on the coast of Canaan around 2066 BC. After Abraham made a covenant with them in Beersheba, "they returned into the land of the Philistines" and "Abraham sojourned in the Philistines' land many days" (Genesis 21:32, 34 KJV). In addition, around 1966 BC, "Isaac went unto Abimelech king of the Philistines unto Gerar" (Genesis 26:1 KJV). Also, the Philistines were said to live on the coast of Canaan around 1446 BC: "Now when Pharaoh had let the people go, God did not lead them by the way of the land of the Philistines" (Exodus 13:17 NASB).

Bible scholars believe that a later Hebrew editor designated earlier peoples as "Philistine" in the Genesis accounts; Philistines lived there in *his* day, so he called that area "the land of the Philistines" to clarify which region the text referred to.

But there's more: The lands and islands of the seafaring

Sea Peoples were *near* Canaan and had already traded with the Canaanites for centuries. No doubt, many had immigrated and settled peacefully among the Canaanites along the coast, especially at Gerar. Since they came from the same lands as the *later* ethnic groups called Philistines, the Bible editor referred to these earlier Sea Peoples as Philistines also—since they *were*.

8

Why would Abimelech fall for the "she's-my-sister" deception twice?

Abraham herded sheep and goats in the Negev, the wilderness south of Canaan. He had to move north during dry years to find pasture and grain supplies in cities there. This brought a new danger: Abraham's wife, Sarah, was so beautiful that he was afraid someone might kill him to take her. So when strangers asked who she was, he'd say she was his sister (Genesis 12:10–20; 20:12–13). In around 2066 BC, Abraham moved to Gerar, where he told the king Abimelech that Sarah was his sister (Genesis 20:1–15).

Circa 1966 BC, after Abraham's death, his son Isaac used the same stratagem for the same reason. "Isaac went unto Abimelech king of the Philistines unto Gerar. . . . And the men of the place asked him of his wife; and he said, She is my sister" (Genesis 26:1, 7 KJV). Abimelech only discovered Isaac's deception after "a long time" (Genesis 26:8–11 KJV).

In both cases, the deception was not only wrong, but unnecessary. But the question many ask is: How can we believe Abimelech would have been dumb enough to fall for the same trick *twice*? Those who believe that the Bible wasn't inspired by God but is merely the product of human authors say that *one* event was carelessly duplicated.

The answer is much more straightforward and simple: The Abimelech who was king of Gerar in Isaac's day was *not* the same Abimelech who had been king in Abraham's day. This was, after all, a hundred years later. He was most likely Abimelech's grandson who had been named after him. Isaac had probably heard his father and mother talk of their ruse, so when he found himself in a similar situation a century later, he decided to try it as well.

9
Were the plagues of Egypt outright miracles, or are there natural explanations?

Scholars have noted that nine of the ten plagues of Exodus were events that naturally occurred in Egypt from late summer to spring. This may be one reason Pharaoh refused to believe they were divine acts. However, other Egyptians *were* convinced that the God of the Hebrews was judging their homeland (Exodus 8:19; 9:20).

Here are the first nine plagues and how they fit in with what often occurred naturally in Egypt:

(1) Plague of blood (7:14–24): the Nile flooded in late summer; heavy rains in the red-soil region of Lake Victoria could have choked the river with bloodred silt.

(2) Plague of frogs (8:1–14): when the fish died (7:21), the frogs fled to land and died.

(3) Plague of gnats (8:16–19): gnats bred in the flooded fields of Egypt in late fall. With no frogs to keep them in check, they (and flies) reproduced in record numbers.

(4) Plague of flies (8:20–32): as the Nile receded, flies began to breed and "dense swarms of flies poured. . . throughout Egypt" (Exodus 8:24 NIV).

(5) Plague on livestock (9:1–7): this may have been a disease carried by biting flies.

(6) Plague of boils (9:8–12): likely also an epidemic transmitted by flies.

(7) Plague of hail (9:13–35): hailstorms happened in January and February.

(8) Plague of locusts (10:1–20): east winds often swept in locusts in March and April.

(9) Plague of darkness (10:21–23): likely caused by a severe *khamsin*, a sandstorm (darkness that could be "felt"—verse 21) that normally occurred every March or April.

These may have been "natural events," but they were miraculously amplified. For example, hailstorms happened, but as God warned, "I will send the worst hailstorm that has ever fallen on Egypt, from the day it was founded till now" (Exodus 9:18 NIV).

And then there's the plague on the firstborn (12:29–30). This selective judgment was clearly an unnatural miracle. After this final plague in April, Pharaoh finally allowed the Hebrews to leave Egypt.

10

Can the Red Sea parting be explained as God using natural phenomena to accomplish divine purposes?

===

We often think that for something to be a miracle, it must defy all known laws of nature. Thus, when we read in Exodus 14:21–22 of God parting the Red Sea and creating walls of water on the right and left hand, we envision water rising vertically, defying gravity. And this is possible for God. After all, He *created* the world and the laws of physics that govern matter.

Moses said, "The floods stood upright like a heap; the depths congealed in the heart of the sea" (Exodus 15:8 NKJV). The word *congealed* means "hardened." That doesn't mean the Red Sea was frozen but that something strange happened to the water. The normal laws of nature were bending to the miracle-working power of God.

God could also have amplified *existing* laws of nature to bring about His desired result. For example, although English Bibles read "Red Sea," the Hebrew words *yam suph* mean "Sea of Reeds"—which seems to refer to a body of water that is shallower yet deep enough to drown in. Thus, many scholars believe that the Hebrews crossed the sea at the present-day Bitter Lakes, just north of the Red Sea.

Another detail to bear in mind: "The LORD caused the sea to go back by a strong east wind all that night, and made the sea dry land, and the waters were divided" (Exodus 14:21 KJV). This "strong east wind" is specifically named as *the* cause. Even today, a phenomena called "wind setdown" (sustained east-west winds) at the Bitter Lakes pushes the waters aside and exposes the lake bottom, allowing Arabs to cross. In Moses' day, God could have stopped the wind abruptly, causing the water to rush back with punishing force upon Pharaoh's chariot army.

No matter *how* God did the miracle, He did it—and the Hebrews escaped Egypt.

11

Do any ancient Egyptian records mention the events of the Exodus?

At least one may do so. A papyrus called the *Admonitions of Ipuwer* describes the land of Egypt in chaos, the Nile turning to blood, and slaves plundering their masters. It also describes the breakdown of law and order, as well as famine following natural catastrophes. It is exactly the situation one would expect to see in Egypt in the months after devastating plagues, widespread destruction of trees and crops, and the wiping out of Egypt's army.

Scholars agree that this papyrus was written no later than the Nineteenth Dynasty. That's the time of Ramesses II, so it could refer to events after an Exodus in 1250 BC. However, most scholars agree that this is a copy of an *earlier* scroll—so it more likely refers to an Exodus in 1446 BC.

Exodus 7:20, 24 (NIV) says: "He raised his staff. . .and

struck the water of the Nile, and all the water was changed into blood. . . . And all the Egyptians dug along the Nile to get drinking water." Meanwhile, Ipuwer 2.10 says: "Indeed, the river is blood, yet men drink of it. Men. . .thirst after water."

Exodus 11:2; 12:36 (NKJV) says, "Let every man ask from his neighbor and every woman from her neighbor, articles of silver and articles of gold. . . . Thus they plundered the Egyptians." Ipuwer 3:3 says, "Indeed, gold and lapis lazuli, silver and turquoise, carnelian and amethyst. . .are strung on the necks of maidservants."

Apart from several parallels to the Bible, Ipuwer describes the state of his country after the power of the government was temporarily broken and anarchy reigned.

Pharaoh Amenhotep II reigned 1454–1419 BC. He conducted ambitious foreign military campaigns until the ninth year of his reign—which (counting 1454 as his first year) would have been 1446 BC, the time of the Exodus. After that, Amenhotep did no more military exploits.

Was the biblical Exodus from Egypt a literal event? If so, when did it take place?

The biblical story of the Exodus of the people of Israel from Egypt was a literal event. The question is, when did it happen? For centuries, biblical historians generally believed it happened around 1446 BC, because 1 Kings 6:1 states that Solomon began to build the Temple in the fourth year of his reign, which was also the 480th year after the Exodus. That was 966 BC, and 966 + 480 = 1446. This means that the invasion of Canaan began forty years after that, in 1406 BC.

In the last century, however, scholars began to favor a later date for the Exodus (around 1250 BC). There are a few reasons for this:

First, the Philistines settled Canaan's coast in 1175 BC. This fits with Shamgar fighting Philistines around 1150 BC (after an Exodus in 1250 BC). But according to an Exodus in 1446 BC, the Philistines would not *arrive* until 150 years after Shamgar. But as has already been explained, pre-Philistine Sea Peoples had already been present in Canaan for hundreds of years.

Second, Exodus 1:11 (NIV) says that the Hebrew slaves "built Pithom and Rameses as store cities for Pharaoh," which seems to indicate that Rameses II was the Pharaoh of the oppression and Exodus. Yet Genesis 47:11 says that Joseph settled his family in "the district of Rameses" four hundred-some years *before* Rameses II. Clearly, this was the home district of the powerful Rameses family.

Third, those who believe in an Exodus in 1250 BC point out that Hazor was burned around 1200 BC. That's true; however, Hazor was *also* burned around 1400 BC—yet became a center of Canaanite power again afterward. Also, the destruction and burning of Jericho fits well with the 1400 BC date, but by 1200 BC Jericho had been in ruins for two hundred years.

Finally, an early Exodus (1446 BC) means not having to explain away the 480 years as "symbolic," and not having to cram all the Judges into nearly half the time.

13

Who actually wrote the Torah, the Books of the Law?

Moses was a real, historical person, and the Torah (the first five books of the Old Testament) repeatedly states that he wrote God's Law (see Exodus 24:3–4; Numbers 33:2; Deuteronomy 31:9, 22, 24).

However, around 1877, the German scholar Julius Wellhausen argued in the Documentary Hypothesis (also called the Wellhausen Hypothesis) that the Law was fabricated (in Moses' name) hundreds of years *after* Moses' death. This hypothesis is also called JEDP, because it states that the Law was created from four sources:

(J) The Jehovah/Yahweh source, written around 950 BC in Judah

(E) The Elohim/El source, written around 850 BC in northern Israel

(D) The Deuteronomic source, written around 600 BC in Judah

(P) The Priestly source, written around 500 BC by priests during the Babylonian Exile

Finally, according to Wellhausen, redactors (editors) combined all the sources, creating the Torah in its present form around 450 BC.

This hypothesis was widely believed until 1987, when biblical scholar R. N. Whybray pointed out the logical fallacies of JEDP. Whybray asked why, if the Yahweh and Elohim sources scrupulously avoided duplication and contradictory themes, did the final editor (trying to create a *believable* "pious fraud") deliberately combine them? Since then, many conflicting, sometimes radically different, theories have replaced Wellhausen's hypothesis.

Not only does the Torah itself state that Moses wrote it, but other early Bible books also refer to the Law existing in *their* day. Joshua "read all the words of the law" (Joshua 8:34–35 NKJV) at the beginning of the conquest of Canaan around 1406 BC. And as he was dying around 970 BC, David told Solomon to "keep the charge of the LORD your God [*Yahweh Elohim*]: to walk in His ways, to keep His statutes, His commandments, His judgments, and His testimonies, as it is written in the Law of Moses" (1 Kings 2:3 NKJV).

14

If Moses wrote the Torah, how can we explain references to events that happened *after* his death?

<hr>

There is no doubt that the Torah includes accounts of events that happened after Moses' death. Conservative scholars agree, for example, that Moses didn't write Deuteronomy 34, which actually describes his death. Obviously, another inspired writer added this passage. And Moses wouldn't have written Numbers 12:3, which proclaims how humble he was. But the fact is, Moses wrote about 99 percent of the Torah.

Here's another example: the author of the book of Joshua tells us, "And the name of Hebron formerly was Kirjath Arba" (Joshua 14:15 NKJV). Yet Genesis 35:27 (NKJV) refers to "Kirjath Arba (that is, Hebron)" and Genesis 13:18 simply calls it "Hebron." Again, God had a later editor add these updates to Genesis.

When were such notes added? Well, two times in Israel's history, their entire alphabet changed, and this required transliterating the scriptures—writing them out in the new alphabets.

The Sinaitic alphabet was commonly used for writing throughout Sinai, Canaan, and Phoenicia in Moses' day, so he probably wrote the Law (in Hebrew) in *that* alphabet. But by around 1000 BC, the Israelites' alphabet had changed and they then used "paleo-Hebrew" letters. (Examples of this are the Gezer calendar, the Siloam inscription, and the Samaritan alphabet.)

The prophet Samuel was alive at that very time; he and Moses were the two godliest men in Israel's history (Jeremiah 15:1; 1 Samuel 3:19–21). The same God who inspired Moses to write the scriptures could have inspired Samuel to transliterate and annotate them.

The second time the Israelites changed their alphabet was around 500–450 BC, when the Aramaic alphabet replaced paleo-Hebrew writing. (This was when the modern, square-lettered Hebrew alphabet came into use.) Again, a wise, godly scholar was alive to transliterate the scriptures. His name was Ezra (see Ezra 7:6; Nehemiah 8:2, 8). He was the most eminent scholar in Israel's history and is believed to have written the books of Ezra and Nehemiah and to have compiled both books of Chronicles.

15
What does the Law of Moses really say about slavery?

Slavery in ancient Israel was not the same as what was practiced in the past in the United States. In America, slave traders actually *sold* men and women who then became the property of their owners. Slaves in America had no rights and couldn't appeal to a judge if their owners overworked or mistreated them. They were often organized into slave gangs and worked under degrading, intolerable conditions.

In ancient Israel, it was usually the decision of the person himself or herself to become a slave. Slaves at this time did this to relieve a situation of severe poverty or to pay off a large debt. When they were desperate for financial security, they would "sell themselves" as servants. For example, Jacob served Laban for fourteen years to pay his bride-price and marry Laban's daughters (Genesis 29:15–30).

The become-a-servant clauses in the Law were written to improve the lot of the impoverished, not to enrich the owners. Slaves had rights, and the Law warned against mistreating them (Leviticus 25:35–43; Exodus 21:20). For example, if a master struck a slave and injured his eye or knocked out a tooth, the slave became free (Exodus 21:26–27). Most slaves were domestic servants, doing the work of a normal laborer. Enterprising slaves could even do business and buy their freedom (Leviticus 25:48–49). After serving six years, Hebrew servants were to be set free, and the master was to send them out with abundant provisions (Deuteronomy 15:12–15).

Furthermore, the laws regulating servitude in Israel were more humane than in the rest of the ancient Middle East. Therefore, Moses' Law specified that if slaves from another country fled to Israel for refuge, the Israelites were not to return them to their former masters but were commanded to allow them to live "wherever they like and in whatever town they choose" (Deuteronomy 23:15–16 NIV).

16

How could Leviticus 11 be the inerrant Word of God when it contains factual misinformation about rabbits?

In Leviticus 11, God told the Israelites, "The rabbit, though it chews the cud, does not have a divided hoof; it is unclean for you" (verse 6 NIV).

However, as Bible critics point out, the rabbit—or "hare" in some translations—does *not* regurgitate its cud and chew it a second time the way cattle and other ruminants do. Though it's a minor detail, there are three such instances in this one chapter. This perplexes many Christians. And the question that comes to mind is, "If the Bible is wrong about *these* things, what *else* is it mistaken about?"

First of all, rabbits *do* chew the cud. So do capybaras, hamsters, and other related species. They just don't get it back in their mouths the way larger, hoofed ruminants do. Many rabbit owners are concerned when they see their pets eating their own feces, but the animals are, in fact, *not* eating feces but *cecotropes*—cuds of half-digested plant matter.

Rabbits have a large cecum situated between their small and large intestines, where bacteria break down plant matter. Many nutrients are not absorbed by the cecum, however, so the chewed food must be expelled, chewed again, and then pass a second time through the intestines. Cecotropes are rich in Vitamin B12, which is essential for a rabbit's health, so once they're expelled through its rectum they're usually immediately re-eaten.

So the rabbit does "chew its cud." Although the modern English word "cud" implies that this already-chewed matter has been regurgitated from a ruminant's stomach directly to its mouth, the original Hebrew word, *gerah*, simply means "chewed food." It doesn't specify the process this *gerah* went through to get back into the rabbit's mouth.

The God who created the rabbit knew this all along. Now you understand why He said that rabbits' meat was unclean.

17
What about the other "errors" in Leviticus 11?

Bible critics say the following verses contain a blatant error: "These are the birds you are to regard as unclean and not eat because they are unclean: the eagle, the vulture, the black vulture. . .and the bat" (Leviticus 11:13, 19 NIV). Most everyone knows that although the bat flies, it's *not* a bird but a mammal. So why does the Bible say it *is?*

In reality, it doesn't. The Hebrew word used here, *oph*, literally means "flyer." Is a bat a flyer? Of course! Most English translations of the Bible use the word "bird"— because all other flyers listed here *are* birds. But it would clear up misunderstandings if they used the more literal word *flyer* instead.

The third "error" in Leviticus 11 is this: "All flying insects that walk on all fours are to be regarded as unclean by you. There are, however, some flying insects that walk on all fours that you may eat: those that have jointed legs for hopping on the ground" (Leviticus 11:20–21 NIV). It then goes on to list locusts, crickets, and grasshoppers as "clean" insects.

All insects, however, have six legs, not four. If God created insects, the argument goes, surely He would have known how many legs He gave them.

The phrase "walk on all fours" is actually a literary expression—taken from observing common four-footed beasts—and means to walk on the ground as opposed to flying. (Remember, it's talking about *flying* insects here.) We use the same expression today. We sometimes say we're "down on all fours" looking for something, even though our hands are technically *not* feet.

The Bible is also making a distinction here between the four normal-sized legs, which are used for nothing but walking, and the larger, hindmost legs of locusts, crickets, and grasshoppers, which, although they're also used for walking, are designed for leaping.

18
How did Moses' staff fit inside the small Ark of the Covenant?

We know from scripture that the Ark of the Covenant was only about three and three-quarters feet long (Exodus 25:10). (A cubit is eighteen inches, so two and a half cubits equals three and three-quarters feet.) The staff that Moses and Aaron used (Exodus 7:19–20; 17:5–6)—which was a standard shepherd's rod—would have been about five to six feet long (Exodus 3:1; 4:1–4). Yet the Bible tells us the staff was able to fit inside the Ark (Hebrews 9:4). How?

The related question is: Why did God tell Moses he couldn't enter the Promised Land just because he lost his temper once? (We *all* lose our temper at times, right?) Well, when the Israelites first started wandering in the desert, God told Moses to strike a rock with the staff and water would come out. Moses obeyed and water gushed out (Exodus 17:1–7).

Nearly forty years later, God commanded Moses to simply *speak* to a rock and water would flow out. But Moses, who was very upset with his people at the time, angrily shouted, "Hear now, you rebels! Must we bring water for you out of this rock?" (Numbers 20:10 NKJV). And instead of just speaking to the rock, he whacked it with the staff. . .*twice*! Water gushed out of the rock, but God said that because Moses didn't believe Him and because he didn't respect Him in front of the Israelites, he couldn't lead them into the Promised Land (see Numbers 20:1–13; Deuteronomy 3:23–27; Psalm 106:32–33).

And that was the very last time Moses used the staff.

Have you guessed by now how a wooden rod measuring five to six feet long could fit inside the Ark of the Covenant? Moses apparently struck the staff against the rock with such fury that it broke in two!

19

Haven't archaeologists proven that Jericho wasn't destroyed in Joshua's day?

When Kathleen Kenyon excavated the city mound of Jericho, Tell es-Sultan, from 1952–58, she determined that the level called City IV had been destroyed around 1550 BC. Radiocarbon dates seemed to back up her conclusion.

However, the Exodus was in 1446 BC, so Jericho would have fallen forty years later, in 1406 BC. In fact, archaeologist John Garstrang came to that very conclusion. When he excavated City IV from 1930–36, he found overwhelming proof that it *was* the Jericho of Joshua's day:

(a) Grain storage jars were full of wheat, barley, dates, and lentils, so Garstrang concluded that Jericho IV was destroyed in early spring, after the harvest. This *was* when Joshua besieged Jericho (Joshua 3:15; 5:10).

(b) The fact that the storage jars were full shows that the city wasn't besieged long. Joshua's siege lasted one week (Joshua 6:3–5).

(c) In nearby tombs, Garstrang discovered scarabs of Pharaohs Hatshepsut (1479–58 BC) and Tuthmosis III (1479–25 BC). He found the *same* type of pottery in the tombs as he did in City IV. This dated the pottery of the destroyed city to 1479–25 BC.

(d) Garstrang found pottery painted to imitate Cypriot bichrome style; this is a recognized indication for the Late Bronze Age (1550–1400 BC).

(e) Houses in Jericho IV were built directly against the

city wall, just as the Bible describes (Joshua 2:15).

(f) City IV was burned; Garstrang found a layer of charcoal, ashes, and fire-reddened bricks more than three feet thick (Joshua 6:24).

(g) The city wall collapsed right down to the base of the tell (Joshua 6:20).

There is no doubt that City IV was the Jericho of Joshua's day. This is established by a weight of evidence that simply cannot be ignored—despite Kenyon's opinions and despite radiocarbon dating. Another key event of that period, the eruption of Santorini, also yields radiocarbon dates that vary widely with Egyptian chronology.

...n't Joshua's wars in Canaan just
...mples of cruel ethnic cleansing?

Canaanite society was so corrupt that God said He was casting them out to make room for the Israelites. In fact, the Canaanites were *so* wicked that the land itself was *vomiting* them out (Leviticus 18:24–25).

God mercifully tried to strike such fear into the Canaanites that those who weren't totally corrupt would flee before Him. That's why He did such tremendous miracles. After God parted the Red Sea and destroyed the chariot armies of Egypt, the most powerful nation on earth, Moses prophesied, "The people will hear and be afraid. . .all the inhabitants of Canaan will melt away. Fear and dread will fall on them" (Exodus 15:14–16 NKJV). And they *did* fear. Rahab told the spies, "Our hearts melted, and no courage remained in any man any longer" (Joshua 2:11 NASB). After God dried the Jordan River "there was no spirit in them any longer" (Joshua 5:1 NKJV).God told the Israelites again and again to "drive them out." He even sent hornets to drive the Canaanites out (Exodus 23:27–31; 34:11; Deuteronomy 7:1). They could have simply fled south to Egypt, and many likely did. In past centuries, tens of thousands of Canaanites *had* migrated to Egypt—and since the Hebrew slaves had left, there was at that very moment a need for laborers.

Sad to say, many Canaanites hardened their hearts and stayed, even though they knew that God Himself, *visibly* traveling with the Israelites (Numbers 14:14), would fight them, even though they knew the Israelites were prepared to wipe them out (Joshua 9:24; 10:1–2). The Canaanites who dug in their heels to fight God Himself brought destruction upon themselves.

21

Did the sun literally stand still in the sky when Joshua prayed for it to?

One day the Amorites surrounded the Israelites' allies at Gibeon, so the Israelites attacked and eventually routed the Amorites. Joshua wanted to finish the battle, so he prayed, "Let the sun stand still over Gibeon, and the moon over the valley of Aijalon." The Bible says, "So the sun stood still and the moon stayed in place until the nation of Israel had defeated its enemies. The sun. . .did not set as on a normal day" (Joshua 10:12–13 NLT).

We know that the sun doesn't orbit the earth but that the earth's rotation makes the sun *appear* to rise and set. So did the world abruptly stop rotating? No. That would have caused global destruction, wiping out all life on earth—the Israelites included. Also, contrary to a popular urban legend, NASA has never discovered "a missing day" in history.

So what really happened at Gibeon? God answered Joshua's prayer, but not the way he'd expected. First of all, the sun was nearly setting when Joshua prayed for it to stand still. (He wouldn't have bothered praying this in the middle of the day with many hours of sunlight still ahead.) Plus, the moon was already shining.

Every day, refraction—in which earth's atmosphere acts like a lens—lengthens daylight by a few minutes. It makes objects appear higher in the sky than they actually are. Refraction causes the sun to be visible moments before it actually rises and causes it to remain "in the sky" for moments after it actually sets below the horizon.

Freakish atmospheric conditions that day caused an extra-ordinary storm, and more Amorites died when huge hail-stones struck them than died in battle (Joshua 10:11). But this event simply cannot be explained by natural phenomena alone. God was evidently manipulating the earth's atmosphere and the laws of nature in a miraculous way.

22

Why does a prominent Israeli archaeologist say that Joshua's conquest never happened?

Israeli archaeologist Israel Finkelstein has demonstrated that around 1200 BC, there was a sudden influx of some twenty-one thousand settlers into the hills of central Canaan. Christians who hold to a "late Exodus" (around 1250 BC) believe these are the Israelites recently come out of Egypt. Finkelstein argues that these newcomers were simply Canaanites who later morphed into the "Israelites." In his opinion, the book of Joshua is a compilation of unrelated "folk memories" about cities destroyed and burned by other peoples at other times.

However, internal evidence shows that the book of Joshua is a historical account, written while eyewitnesses were still living (Joshua 6:25). As we have shown, Jericho *was* destroyed around 1400 BC, and history tells us that around 1400 BC was one of three dates when Hazor was destroyed. Jericho and Hazor were just about the only cities Joshua destroyed and burned, so we shouldn't expect evidence of Canaan-wide destruction. The Israelites' normal practice was to defeat a Canaanite army then move into the intact cities, houses, and lands (Deuteronomy 6:10–11).

Another point: Joshua 11:16 (NLT) says, "So Joshua conquered the entire region—the hill country, the entire Negev. . .the western foothills, the Jordan Valley, the mountains of Israel, and the Galilean foothills." Yet despite their stunning initial victories, due to later disobedience, the Israelites weren't able to *hold* all this land. Even though they conquered and burned Hazor, within a few decades it was again the center of a Canaanite kingdom (Joshua 11:12–13; Judges 4:1–3). They also conquered Jerusalem, yet it remained a Canaanite stronghold for hundreds more years (Judges 1:8; 2 Samuel 5:6–7; see also Judges 1:19–35).

Even twenty-five years after the conquest, when the Israelites were still largely obedient, God told Joshua that "there remains *very much* land yet to be possessed" (Joshua 13:1 NKJV, emphasis added).

23
Wasn't El (the name for the Hebrew God) originally a Canaanite god?

No. The opposite is true: Much of the ancient Middle East—including the Canaanites—recognized El, the true God, as the Creator God. They recognized El as the original and highest God but early on began to see Him as distant and uncaring. So they developed a mythology in which He spawned seventy sons and daughters who were more accessible.

The world gained a clearer picture of the Canaanite pantheon in 1928, when clay tablets were discovered in Ras Shamra (ancient Ugarit). These tablets described Canaanite beliefs in detail. According to "The Baal Cycle," Baal was chief of the gods under El. Canaanites worshiped Baal most of all, as they believed he had power over essential things such as rain, crops, and fertility. Baal's wife was the goddess Asherah, and Canaanites worshiped them both in lascivious rites.

You can see how tempting it would have been for the Israelites to turn from worshipping God, El Most High (Genesis 14:19), also called El-Shaddai and Elohim, to worshipping Baal and Asherah—which is exactly what they *did* for much of their history (Judges 3:7; 1 Kings 18:19). This was despite the fact that Moses had commanded them to worship the Lord God (*Yahweh Elohim*) alone, and to utterly demolish the altars and idols of the Canaanite gods (Deuteronomy 12:2–3).

Even when the Israelites worshipped Yahweh, however,

they often slipped into syncretism, worshiping Baal, too (1 Kings 18:21). They even assigned Baal's wife to God. An ancient inscription found in Khirbet el-Kom near Hebron, reads: "Blessed be Uriyahu by Yahweh and by his Asherah."

Some people try to cite this to say God has a wife. In reality, all it proves is what the Bible declares: that the Israelites often disobeyed Him by worshipping Asherah, even in the very temple of Yahweh (2 Kings 21:7).

24
What do the Amarna Letters
tell us about the Hebrews in Canaan?

The Amarna Letters, discovered in Egypt, are an archive of clay tablets sent from kings in Canaan to the Pharaohs. They are basically the Canaanite side of the story. Written from the 1350s–30s BC, they contain desperate appeals for Egyptian archers to stop the attacks of the Habiru/Hapiru, recognizably the Hebrews. In letter 288, Abdi-Heba, king of Jerusalem, wrote Pharaoh that "the Hapiru have taken the very cities of the king," and warned, "If there are no archers this year, all the lands of the king, my lord, are lost" (see Judges 1:8).

In the early period of the Judges, following the death of Joshua, the Israelites in Canaan didn't stand out too much because they had largely adopted the Canaanites' housing styles, pottery, customs, and even their gods. They formed alliances with them (Judges 2:2–3) and even intermarried. "Thus the children of Israel dwelt among the Canaanites. . . . And they took their daughters to be their wives, and gave their daughters to their sons; and they served their gods" (Judges 3:5–6 NKJV).

Although they were in danger of becoming assimilated, for the most part they retained their Hebrew identity and resorted to a mixture of warfare against—and alliances with—the Canaanites. Whenever they gained the upper hand, they made the Canaanites pay tribute (Judges 1:28). This is the kind of complex situation that the Amarna Letters describe in the decades following Joshua's death.

One of the most interesting characters was Labayu, ruler of Shechem. Other Canaanites accused him of allying with the Habiru. Abdi-Heba declared that Labayu had handed over Shechem to them. Biridiya, prince of Megiddo, complained that Labayu's sons had hired Habiru mercenaries to war against him. When Labayu wrote Pharaoh, however, he innocently denied knowing that one of his sons consorted with the Habiru.

25

Are there any other proofs that the Israelites lived in Canaan early on?

Early in his reign, Pharaoh Merneptah led a punitive raid into the land of Canaan, and his victory stele (inscribed around 1209 BC) names the cities he conquered. It also states, "Israel is laid waste; its seed is no more." This is the earliest mention of Israel in Egyptian records. This "seed" likely refers to Israel's crops being burned, a common practice at the time. Israel was just a confederation of tribes during the period of the Judges, and Merneptah's stele confirms this. His hieroglyphics specify that Israel was a "foreign people," not a "country."

Also, research by Israeli archaeologist Israel Finkelstein shows that around 1200 BC, less than a decade after the Egyptian raid, there was a sudden influx of some twenty-one thousand people into the central hills of Canaan. Almost overnight, 250 new settlements appeared in these previously uninhabited highlands. The distinctive feature of these settlements was the absence of pig bones—as we know, Israelites were commanded not to eat pork (Leviticus 11:7).

Based upon an Exodus in 1446 BC, 1200 BC was the *exact time* that Midianite hordes began overrunning the plains and valleys of Canaan and Israel.* "Because the power of Midian was so oppressive, the Israelites prepared shelters for themselves in mountain clefts, caves and strongholds" (Judges 6:2 NIV). Many took refuge in the hills and began permanent settlements.

*Jephthah said it had been three hundred years since Israel had conquered the land that Ammon now claimed (Judges 11:25–26). Israel conquered that land in 1406 BC, so Ammon's eighteen-year war began in 1106 BC (Judges 10:8–9). If you add the numbers in Judges 10:3; 10:2; 9:22; 8:28; and 6:1, they take you back ninety-five years from 1106 BC to the beginning of the Midianite raids in 1201 BC. The Israelite retreat to the hills began then.

26

Who was high priest during Saul's reign, Abiathar or Ahimelek?

When the Pharisees criticized Jesus and His disciples for "working" on the Sabbath by plucking heads of grain to eat, Jesus replied, "Have you never read what David did when he and his companions were hungry and in need? In the days of Abiathar the high priest, he entered the house of God and ate the consecrated bread" (Mark 2:25–26 NIV).

However, the story Jesus was referring to says, "David went to Nob, to Ahimelek the priest" (1 Samuel 21:1 NIV) and Ahimelek—not his son Abiathar—gave David and his men consecrated bread (1 Samuel 21:2–6). So did Mark make a mistake? Did he misquote Jesus?

After David was at Nob, Saul ordered Ahimelek and his entire extended family (eighty-five priests, all told) to be killed. Only Ahimelek's son Abiathar escaped (1 Samuel

22:9–21). After *that*, yes, Abiathar was high priest. But was he already high priest on the day David arrived there? It seems so.

At that time, Ahimelek and *all* eighty-five men in his extended family were "priests" (1 Samuel 22:11), so calling him "Ahimelek the priest" simply states the obvious. It doesn't mean he was still the *high* priest, the officiating priest. Very likely he was retired from active duty at that point and Abiathar now held the position. That Ahimelek gave David consecrated bread shows that, as former high priest, he still had authority.

A similar situation occurred when the priest Eli was old: his sons Hophni and Phinehas were now the officiating priests, were called the "priests of the LORD" (1 Samuel 1:3 NIV), and were doing the actual sacrifices. Eli was no longer acting high priest, yet he still had the authority to bless the Israelites, and Hannah presented Samuel to Eli, not to his sons (1Samuel 1:17, 25).

27
How could Saul *not* have recognized David, his own armor-bearer?

Many people are mystified when they read King Saul's reaction as David went to fight Goliath. Saul asked his army commander, "Abner, whose son is this youth?" Abner didn't know, so when David came back after killing Goliath, Saul asked, "Whose son are you, young man?" (1 Samuel 17:55, 58 NKJV).

However, in the *previous* chapter, Saul knew David's name, loved him, and had made him his personal armor-bearer. Not only that, but David played music for him whenever he was troubled. How could Saul possibly *not* have recognized David? Bible critics, therefore, say that the sixteenth and seventeenth chapters of 1 Samuel give conflicting accounts of how Saul and David first met.

Some Christians reply that Saul, distressed by a troubling spirit (1 Samuel 16:14), suffered some kind of dementia and couldn't remember who David was. (But Abner, *too*?) The answer, however, had to do with a binding declaration Saul had just made.

Saul had made a vow regarding Goliath: "The man who kills him the king will enrich with great riches, will give him his daughter, and give his father's house exemption from taxes in Israel" (1 Samuel 17:25 NKJV). Saul later gave David his daughter—and probably riches—but he'd also sworn to "give his father's house exemption from taxes." So who *was* his father? Saul needed to know. Note that David answered

Saul's question not by giving his *own* name, but by saying, "I am the son of your servant Jesse the Bethlehemite" (1 Samuel 17:58 NKJV).

Previously, Saul had allowed David to go back and forth to his father's house—which is why David had just arrived from Bethlehem—but that now changed (1 Samuel 18:2). David was now in Saul's full-time employ.

28
What archaeological support has been found for the Bible's accounts of Israel's kings and their wars?

Archaeology abundantly supports the Bible's accounts of Israel's monarchy and its wars.

The Bible states, "Now Mesha king of Moab raised sheep, and he had to pay the king of Israel a tribute of a hundred thousand lambs and the wool of a hundred thousand rams. But after Ahab died, the king of Moab rebelled against the king of Israel. So at that time King Joram set out from Samaria and mobilized all Israel" (2 Kings 3:4–6 NIV).

In 1868, the Mesha Stele was found in Jordan. It is Mesha's account of his rebellion, dedicated to his god, Chemosh. It states, in part: "I am Mesha, son of Kemosh, king of Moab. And I built this high place to Kemosh to commemorate deliverance from all the kings. . . . Omri was king of Israel, and he oppressed Moab for many days. . .and his son [Ahab] replaced him; and he also said, 'I will oppress Moab.' But I was victorious over him and his house."

Also, the Bible states that Ben-Hadad was king of Aram, that the prophet Elisha anointed Hazael king, and that Hazael then assassinated Ben-Hadad and ruled in his place (2 Kings 8:7–15). An inscription by Shalmaneser, king of Assyria says, "I fought with Ben-Hadad. I accomplished his defeat. Hazael, son of a nobody, seized his throne."

Other Assyrian monuments add new details that dovetail with what the Bible tells us: Jehoram was the grandson of Omri (1 Kings 16:29; 2 Kings 3:1) and the Black Obelisk, found in Shalmaneser's palace, states: "The tribute of Iaua mar Hu-umrii [Jehoram son of Omri]: I have received from him silver, gold, a bowl of gold, chalices of gold, tumblers of gold, buckets of gold, tin, a scepter for the king, and spears." [Some believe *Iaua* was Jehu, who slew Jehoram and was the next king of Israel (2 Kings 9)].

29
Does Psalm 137 say evil men should be *happy* as they kill infants?

This passage has long disturbed believers: "Daughter Babylon, doomed to destruction, happy is the one who repays you according to what you have done to us. Happy is the one who seizes your infants and dashes them against the rocks" (Psalm 137:8–9 NIV).

In Jeremiah's day, Israel had rebelled against God so He allowed the Babylonians to attack them. Jeremiah wept in anguish as his people were slain and their children collapsed from hunger (Lamentations 2:11). The Lord had sent the Babylonians to judge the people of Israel for their sins, but their excessive cruelty was *not* part of His plan. God said, "I was angry with my chosen people and punished them by letting them fall into your hands. But you, Babylon, showed them no mercy" (Isaiah 47:6 NLT).

The Babylonians then mercilessly demanded that the grieving exiles entertain them with happy songs: "our tormentors demanded songs of joy" (Psalm 137:3 NIV). The point of this psalm is that just as the Babylonian tormentors got perverse pleasure from slaying the Jews and then forcing the traumatized survivors to sing joyful tunes, *their* enemies would get a twisted sense of happiness out of slaying them— men, women, and children. Warfare back then was barbaric and cruel, and the defenseless and innocent weren't spared (2 Kings 8:12).

God didn't desire Babylon's enemies to be that cruel, let

alone be happy doing it. The psalmist was simply repeating what the prophet Isaiah had said those enemies *would* do: "A prophecy against Babylon. . . . Their infants will be dashed to pieces before their eyes. . . . I will stir up against them the Medes. . . . Their bows will strike down the young men; they will have no mercy on infants" (Isaiah 13:1, 16–18 NIV).

The Babylonians were ruthless and cruel, and God knew that their enemies were just as ruthless and cruel as they were.

30
What does the Bible really say about the shape of the earth?

Some skeptics believe the Bible says the world is flat with four corners. That, they say, is proof that the Bible wasn't inspired by God (who, according to them, probably doesn't exist anyway) but was written by mere men with primitive, unscientific worldviews. The problem with this position, however, is that nowhere does the Bible *say* the world is flat. This *was* the general worldview of people of that day, and the Hebrews may have had this misconception. But it isn't stated in the Bible. In fact, the scriptures taught way back in 700 BC that the world is round:

"Have you not known? Have you not heard? Has it not been told you from the beginning? Have you not understood from the foundations of the earth? It is He who sits above the circle of the earth, and its inhabitants are like grasshoppers" (Isaiah 40:21–22 NKJV). A circle is as round as things get.

As for the Mesopotamian belief that the world was a raft floating on the waters, the Bible stated this scientific reality in 1,500 BC: "He [God] spreads out the northern skies over empty space; he suspends the earth over nothing" (Job 26:7 NIV).

Still, the critics argue, the Bible *does* mention "the four corners of the earth" (Isaiah 11:12 KJV). However, the Hebrew word translated "corners" is *kanaph*, which literally means "wings." Clearly, this is symbolic language used to describe the four directions—north, south, east, and west. The same word is used in Ezekiel 7:2 (KJV), which refers to "the four corners of the land" of Israel. Yet no critics would argue that the Israelites believed their country was a square, or that there were four giant wings on the borders of their nation.

31
What, if anything, does the Bible say about life on other planets— or other solar systems or galaxies?

When God created our sun and planet, "he made the stars also" (Genesis 1:16 KJV). Astronomers estimate that there are 200 billion to 400 billion stars in our Milky Way Galaxy alone. And they guesstimate that there are some 170 billion galaxies in the universe. You do the math—that's a *lot* of stars! It shows us how astonishingly creative God really is.

Scientists have discovered hundreds of planets orbiting nearby stars and calculate that odds are our galaxy has some 50 billion planets, of which 500 million are within the habitable zone of their star. Now, if 500 million planets (just in our galaxy) can potentially support life, isn't it reasonable to believe that the Planet Earth just might not be the only inhabited world? Are we so special after all?

Some note that God "stretches out the heavens. . .like a tent to dwell in" (Isaiah 40:22 NKJV) and argue that He expressly created habitable planets like Earth to be inhabited (Isaiah 45:18). But we still can't say for sure whether or not life exists elsewhere. But if it *does* exist, it was God (through Jesus Christ) who created it: "All things were made through Him, and without Him nothing was made that was made" (John 1:3 NKJV).

This brings up another question: If there *is* life elsewhere in the universe, is it fallen like earth's humanity and in need of salvation? As some have asked, "Did Jesus die for Klingons, too?" Well, we can't know whether or not hypothetical beings on other planets are fallen. But we *do* know that every sentient being in existence will one day worship Jesus: "that at the name of Jesus every knee should bow, of those in heaven, and of those on earth. . .and that every tongue should confess that Jesus Christ is Lord" (Philippians 2:10–11 NKJV).

The planet Earth may or may not be unique in its ability to support life—but Jesus Christ is *definitely* unique!

32
Why do Matthew and Luke give different genealogies for Jesus?

Matthew listed Jesus' ancestors at the beginning of his Gospel. This was important, because he was writing for a Jewish audience, and the Jews knew that the Messiah would be descended from King David. Matthew's purpose of including Jesus' pedigree was to confirm that He *was* "the Son of David" (Matthew 1:1 NKJV).

Matthew gave Jesus' lineage beginning with Abraham, but Luke, who was a Gentile, traced Jesus' lineage all the way back to Adam to show His link with *all* humanity. From Abraham to David, the two lists are almost exactly the same. However, beginning with King David, they list *very* different ancestors. Compare these:

David, Solomon, Rehoboam, Abijah, Asa, Jehoshaphat, etc. (Matthew 1:6–8)

David, Nathan, Mattathah, Menan, Melea, Eliakim, etc. (Luke 3:30–31)

The lists continue to differ all the way down the line to Joseph's immediate ancestors:

Achim, Eliud, Eleazar, Matthan, Jacob, Joseph (Matthew 1:14–16)

Janna, Melchi, Levi, Matthat, Heli, Joseph (Luke 3:23–24)

Why the differences? Well, Matthew, following required Jewish format, listed the genealogy of Jesus' earthly father, Joseph—even though he went on to state that Joseph was *not* Jesus' natural, biological father (Matthew 1:18). Note that all the royal kings of Judah were Joseph's ancestors. He was not only of the *lineage* of David, but of the "*house* and lineage of David" (Luke 2:4 NKJV, emphasis added).

But for Jesus to be physically descended from King David, and not simply be adopted by one of his descendants, His mother, Mary, *also* had to be "of the lineage of David." And she was. Jews didn't cite women's genealogies, but Mary's father, Heli, kept track of *his*, and he (and therefore Mary) was *also* descended from David, through one of David's younger sons, Nathan (1 Chronicles 3:5). It is therefore Mary's genealogy that Luke records.

33
Were huge crowds of followers and fans a danger to Jesus?

Jesus was so wildly popular during His earthly ministry that crowd control was sometimes a serious issue. Often when He was in a house or went walking in public, people crowded thickly around Him (Mark 2:1–2; 5:24). It got to be such a problem that after a while He could no longer openly enter certain cities (Mark 1:45).

Jesus had a tremendous reputation as a healer, so people who were sick pushed and pressed through packed crowds so they could touch Him and be healed (Mark 3:10). At one point "a great multitude, when they heard how many things He was doing, came to Him. So He told His disciples that a small boat should be kept ready for Him because of the multitude, lest they should crush Him" (Mark 3:8–9 NKJV).

Got that? Jesus stood with His back to the lake, facing the crowds ringing Him on the shore, with a small boat behind Him. Probably a couple of disciples stood beside this boat and "kept ready" to launch out. In case the crowd got too excited and impatient and all surged forward to touch Him at once, Jesus had an escape plan: He would jump into the boat and push out to sea.

At one point, that's what He did. Before He had twelve disciples to help with crowd control, Jesus was teaching and "great crowds pressed in on him to listen to the word of God." As a precautionary measure, Jesus got into Simon Peter's boat and had him push out a ways from the shore (Luke 5:1–3 NLT).

It wasn't just Jesus they nearly crushed, but each other. One time, "an innumerable multitude of people had gathered together, so that they trampled one another" (Luke 12:1 NKJV). Hopefully, only people's toes got trampled.

34
How long after Jesus' death and resurrection were the Gospels written?

Many scholars state that none of the Gospels was written before AD 70, some forty years after Jesus ascended back to heaven. This is based upon two assumptions: (a) the Romans destroyed Jerusalem in AD 70, but skeptics argue that the Gospels containing Jesus' prophecies about that event (Matthew 24:1–2; Luke 21:20–24) must have been composed *after* the fact. (b) As to why Matthew (an eyewitness) and Luke (who interviewed eyewitnesses) would have waited so long to write their narratives, critics insist that others actually penned their Gospels.

However, Church tradition attributes the first three Gospels to Matthew, Mark, and Luke and states that they were written early. Internal evidence points to the same. For example, Luke's Gospel and the book of Acts are both dedicated to Theophilus (Luke 1:3; Acts 1:1). Now, we know that Luke wrote Acts before AD 62, when Paul was released from his first imprisonment, because the book ends with Paul still under house arrest (Acts 28:30–31).

In Acts, Luke refers to his "former book" (Acts 1:1 NIV). He therefore likely wrote his Gospel before AD 60. Luke also states that "many" had written Gospels before him (Luke 1:1), so Mark and Matthew also likely would have been written before AD 60.

Matthew's Gospel was written for Jews, and "Matthew, who had at first preached to the Hebrews, when he was about to go to other peoples, committed his Gospel to writing" (Eusebius, *Ecclesiastical History*, Book 3, Chapter 24).

The apostles were still in Jerusalem in AD 49–50, because Acts 15:2, 4, and 6 tell us that the "apostles and elders" met Paul then. However, when Paul went to Jerusalem in AD 57, he met "James, and all the elders" (Acts 21:17–18 NIV) but no apostles. They had left to fulfill the Great Commission. So Matthew composed his Gospel around AD 50–56.

35
Which Gospel was written first—Matthew or Mark?

The Church fathers believed that Matthew wrote his Gospel first and that Mark edited down Matthew's work to the bare-bones story. However, it's likely that Mark was closer to the original story since in places the sense of the underlying Aramaic words shows through in his Greek text.

Mark is the shortest Gospel of the four. It focuses on the basic story of Jesus with almost none of the parables or stories found in Matthew and Luke. Mark is only 661 verses long, yet 606 of those verses (often quoted word for word) are found in Matthew. In other words, 92 percent of Mark appears in Matthew. In addition, 350 verses from Mark appear with little change in Luke. That is why many Bible scholars believe that Matthew and Luke based their Gospels on Mark's text. This theory is called "Markan priority."

However, it's unlikely that the task of first organizing and writing Jesus' biography would have been left to Mark, since Jesus had appointed twelve apostles whose time was devoted "continually to. . .the ministry of the word" (Acts 6:2, 4 NKJV). Mark was not among the Twelve. *They* knew the facts best and had been commissioned to bear witness to Christ (Acts 1:21–22). Very likely, the apostles wrote down the basic framework of Jesus' words and deeds early on, and then Mark, Matthew, and Luke all independently based their Gospels on *this* original document, with Matthew and Luke adding more of Jesus' sayings and parables from other sources.

What other sources? Papias (AD 70–163) wrote, "Matthew compiled the *Logia* in the Hebrew [that is, Aramaic] speech, and everyone translated them as best he could." *Logia* means "oracles," and this is thought to refer to an original Aramaic collection of Jesus' sayings and parables. Scholars commonly call this "Q" for the German word *quelle*, which means "source."

36
Why do some people believe the Gospels were based on already-written records?

It makes eminent sense that when Matthew, Mark, and Luke wrote their Gospels, they based them on an already-written story framework to which they added stories, quotes, and parables from a second written resource (commonly called Q). John did not use that framework when he wrote his Gospel but drew heavily from *other* written sources.

Many Christians hesitate to believe in Q because it's often endorsed by unbelieving scholars. Yet the existence of a written collection of sayings would ensure the accuracy and inerrancy of the Bible's text. If there wasn't an early written record of Jesus' sayings, how could Matthew—some twenty-five years later—quote lengthy chunks of Jesus' sayings in chapters 5, 6, and 7? And how could John—some sixty years after Jesus' death, burial, resurrection, and ascension—quote Jesus verbatim in chapters 14, 15, 16, and 17? It's important that we have the *actual* words of Jesus in passages such as John 14:6—not half-remembered summaries or paraphrases.

Now, some Jews could, over a period of years, memorize large portions of the Law—but they had a written text to constantly refer to. How do you memorize a sermon, though, while someone's *giving* it? Some Christians quote Jesus' promise that the Holy Spirit would "bring to your remembrance all things that I said to you" (John 14:26 NKJV). They believe God did a miracle each time the apostles sat down to write. That's possible. Nevertheless, reusable wax-covered writing tablets existed long before AD 30, as did professional scribes trained to take notes in shorthand.

Of all Jesus' apostles, who was most likely that scribe? Matthew, of course, since he'd been an official tax collector for the Romans—a job that required him to be fluent in both Greek and Aramaic, and to write down very accurate, detailed records.

37
When did the disciples first *know* that Jesus was the Messiah and the Son of God?

One day, John the Baptist's disciples heard him declare that Jesus was the Lamb of God and the Messiah (John 1:29–36). Two of those disciples then spent hours talking with Jesus. Andrew came away so impressed that he told his brother Simon, "We have found the Messiah." The next day, Nathanael exclaimed, "Rabbi, you are the Son of God—the King of Israel!" (John 1:41, 49 NLT). Bible scholars tell us this happened in the fall of AD 26, at the beginning of Jesus' ministry.

However, in the spring of AD 29, when Simon Peter declared, "You are the Christ, the Son of the living God," Jesus said, "Blessed are you, Simon Bar-Jonah, for flesh and blood has not revealed this to you, but My Father who is in heaven" (Matthew 16:16–17 NKJV). *That* sounds like Simon Peter was the *first* to realize Jesus was the Christ, and only after having been with Him for two and a half years. So which Gospel is right?

Both are. In Jesus' day, Jews eagerly expected the arrival of the Messiah, and Jesus' disciples followed Him because they believed He was the One. Even the crowds speculated that He was the Messiah (John 7:25–26, 31, 40–41). To avoid being mobbed by admirers or stoned by enemies, however, Jesus refrained from publicly declaring His true identity, leading many people to wonder just *who* He was (Matthew 16:13–14).

Because Jesus wasn't working to overthrow the Roman government, like many Jews thought the Messiah would, John the Baptist—who had called Jesus the Messiah—asked, "Are you the Messiah we've been expecting, or should we keep looking for someone else?" (Matthew 11:3 NLT).

Even many of Jesus' disciples gave up hope, but Simon declared, "We have come to believe and to know that you are the Holy One of God" (John 6:69 NIV). Then Simon Peter's declaration three months later (in Matthew 16) was a reaffirmation of the disciples' unswerving faith in Jesus.

38
Did the early Church deliberately change the original Greek words to make Jesus look better?

In his book *Misquoting Jesus*, Bart Ehrman presents Mark 1:41 as proof that editors deliberately doctored the text. In question are the Greek words *splangnistheis* ("feeling compassion") and *orgistheis* ("becoming angry"). In almost every Greek manuscript, *splangnistheis* appears in Mark 1:41. Thus, most Bibles read that Jesus "felt compassion" when a leper came to Him saying, "If you are willing, you can make me clean" (Mark 1:40 NIV). As the 1984 version of the NIV reads, "Filled with compassion, Jesus reached out his hand and touched the man."

But in *one* Greek manuscript, Codex Bezae, the word *orgistheis* appears, so that when the leper asked Jesus to heal him, Jesus became angry. . .*then* healed him. Wanting to reflect the "original" Greek text, the 2011 version of the NIV reads, "Jesus was indignant. He reached out his hand and touched the man."

It frankly makes no difference to our understanding of Jesus' nature which word was original. We can certainly understand Jesus having compassion on a poor leper (Matthew 14:14; 20:34). On the other hand, Mark doesn't hesitate to show Jesus becoming indignant or angry on other occasions (Mark 3:5; 10:14).

However, there's such a difference between *orgistheis* and *splangnistheis* that critics argue that the text was blatantly changed to make Jesus look better. Actually, it's more likely that it's an innocent scribal error. A Jewish Christian fluent in both Aramaic and Greek, when copying Mark's Gospel, would have realized that the underlying Aramaic word *ethra'em* (He was enraged) is very easily confused with *ethraham* (He had pity). Concluding that a translation error had been made, he changed the Greek word accordingly.

After examining all the evidence, Dr. Daniel B. Wallace, an evangelical New Testament Studies professor at Dallas Theological Seminary, came to believe that the case is strong for Jesus having pity, but that the evidence weighs slightly more toward Jesus being angry. (For more information, see the online NET Bible.)

39
Why do some events appear in different order in the Gospels?

Bible students have realized for two thousand years that although Matthew, Mark, and Luke often relate the same incidents in the same order, they don't *always* do so.

For example, Matthew's Gospel relates these events in *this* order: (1) Jesus calls Matthew to follow; (2) He heals a woman and raises a dead girl; (3) He heals the man with a withered hand (Matthew 9:9–13,18–26; 12:9–14). Mark, however, relates the same events in *this* order: (1) Jesus calls Matthew to follow; (2) He heals the man with a withered hand; (3) He heals a woman and raises a dead girl (Mark 2:13–17; 3:1–6; 5:21–43).

The major events of Jesus' ministry are in the same chronological order, but sometimes the minor incidents have been arranged in different orders.

What is more amazing is that when the Gospels relate the same incident or saying, they repeat it almost word for word—sometimes *exactly* word for word (compare Matthew 3:7–10 with Luke 3:7–9.) This is why Matthew, Mark, and Luke are called the Synoptic Gospels. The word *synoptic* means "seen together." The first three gospels are called the Synoptic Gospels because they contain so many parallel texts.

These short, self-contained stories are called *pericopes*, a Greek word that means "a cutting out." It appears that these pericopes were written and compiled early on and that the Gospel writers then chose the stories they wanted—generally following the same timeline, but sometimes rearranging the material for editorial purposes, to suit their intended audience. In a sense, this *is* what happened, but God guided the process.

As the church father Tertullian (AD 160–220) said, "Never mind if there does occur some variation in the order of their narratives, provided that there be agreement in the essential matter of the faith" (*Against Marcion*, IV, 2).

40

How accurate are the Gospel accounts of the words Jesus said?

Often when the Synoptic Gospels relate the same incident, they give different details. This is to be expected and is not a problem, as these are just different views of the same event. Sometimes, however, the Gospels vary slightly as to what Jesus said. The meaning of what He says is the same, but the words used are sometimes a bit different. So the question some people ask is this: Do the Gospels record the *exact* words Jesus said, or only a close approximation?

For example, when Jesus and the apostles were caught in the middle of a storm so terrible that the Twelve thought they were about to perish, Jesus rebuked the wind and the waves—which instantly calmed. Matthew tells us that after Jesus calmed the storm, He asked, "You of little faith, why are you so afraid?" (Matthew 8:26 NIV). Mark reports that He asked, "Why are you so afraid? Do you still have no faith?" (Mark 4:40 NIV), while Luke tells us that Jesus asked simply, "Where is your faith?" (Luke 8:25 NIV).

A careful reading of all three stories, however, shows that Jesus asked the question in Matthew just *before* He calmed the storm. Then, *after* he'd done the miracle He asked, "Why are you so afraid? Do you still have no faith?" Since the disciples were too astonished to answer Him, it's easy to see Jesus sadly asking again, "Where is your faith?"

The differences in what the disciples shouted to Jesus are easy to explain. There were, after all, twelve of them in the boat with Jesus and they believed they were in terrible danger and were frightened out of their wits. They undoubtedly said all the things Matthew, Mark, and Luke record them saying, and probably quite a bit more as well (Matthew 8:25; Mark 4:38; Luke 8:24).

41
Did Jesus preach the Sermon on the Mount on a hilltop or down on a plain?

Many people wonder why there are differences between Matthew's and Luke's accounts of the famous "Sermon on the Mount." Here's how each of them begin:

- "Now when [Jesus] saw the crowds, he went up on a mountainside and sat down. His disciples came to him, and he began to teach them. He said: 'Blessed are the poor in spirit, for theirs is the kingdom of heaven'" (Matthew 5:1–3 NIV).
- "He went down with them and stood on a level place. A large crowd of his disciples was there and a great number of people. . . . Looking at his disciples, he said: 'Blessed are you who are poor, for yours is the kingdom of God'" (Luke 6:17, 20 NIV).

Matthew tells us Jesus was sitting on a mountainside, while Luke says He was standing on a plain. In addition,

Luke reports that Jesus gave this sermon immediately after choosing the twelve apostles, whereas in Matthew's Gospel, Jesus didn't choose His apostles until *several* chapters after this sermon. Also, although they both begin with the Beatitudes, Matthew's version is much longer, stretching out over three chapters. Luke not only omits much material, but he scatters parts of it throughout his Gospel (see Luke 11:2–4; 12:22–31, 33–34).

Finally, Jesus' wording, although similar in Matthew and Luke, has many striking differences, as even His brief opening words show.

There is no need to attempt to harmonize them into one event. The multi-subject Sermon on the Mount in Matthew 5–7 is commonly understood to be the *heart* of Jesus' teaching. Therefore, as He traveled around Judea and Galilee, He would have repeated these core messages again and again, to new crowds in different towns, villages, and open-air settings. Yes, He taught *other* principles and told *other* parables as well, but these were probably some of His most oft-repeated teachings.

42
Why does Luke give the wrong date for when Quirinius was governor?

Luke wrote, "In those days Caesar Augustus issued a decree that a census should be taken of the entire Roman world. (This was the first census that took place while Quirinius was governor of Syria.)" (Luke 2:1–2 NIV). Jesus was born in 4 BC, so Caesar's decree would have happened then. The problem, however, is that Quirinius was governor of Syria from AD 6–9, when he conducted a census, which was so unpopular that it sparked a Jewish revolt (Acts 5:37).

Pope Gregory XIII's aides made a mistake when calculating our modern calendar. We now know that Jesus was born four years earlier—hence He was actually born in 4 BC. Some people wonder if Luke also got his dates mixed up, or his information wrong.

The Greek for this passage literally reads, "*This enrollment first was governing Syria Cyrenius.*" Therefore, the NIV footnotes suggest an alternate translation: "This census took place before Quirinius was governor of Syria." In other words, Luke—who wrote both the Gospel of Luke and the book of Acts—was clarifying for his readers that this was *not* the more recent census under Quirinius but an earlier one.

Many Christians, however, believe that Quirinius was possibly governor of Syria *twice*—first in 4 BC and again in AD 6–9—and that he conducted a census both times. History is silent on whether Quirinius was governor of Syria twice, but it seems unlikely.

One thing that seems certain is that no surviving Roman records speak of an empire-wide census taking place in 4 BC. But did such records once exist? The Latin Church Father Tertullian (AD 160–220) says that this earlier census indeed took place, and that it was documented in the archives in Rome (*Against Marcion* 4:7). These records no longer exist, but according to Tertullian, they were extant in his day.

Luke's accuracy has been questioned when his accounts disagreed with those of historians, but every time, new archaeological evidence vindicated his statements.

43
Why does John's Gospel differ so much from the other Gospels? Is it a later forgery?

John's Gospel doesn't recount several of the events of Jesus' life found in the other Gospels, plus it recounts many incidents and conversations the Synoptic Gospels don't. But John doesn't contradict Matthew, Mark, or Luke. Rather, his Gospel is a rich source of information that fills in many gaps in the story and greatly clarifies the timeline.

John emphasizes the deity of Christ to a much greater extent than the other Gospel writers. While this theme *is* found in the Synoptics, John boldly states that "the Word was God" and "the Word became flesh" (John 1:1, 14 NIV). Saint Jerome wrote that one of the reasons John wrote his

Gospel was to counter the heresies of the Ebionites—who taught that Jesus was the Messiah but was the natural son of Joseph who *became* the Son of God at His baptism.

John's Gospel is believed to have been written around AD 85–90. Scholars once argued that its theology was so developed that someone else pretending to be an eyewitness must have written it much later. But in 1920, a fragment of the Gospel of John (the *Rylands Library Papyrus P52*), which dated to AD 117–138, was found. If copies already existed then, the original must date even earlier. Also, the author *was* very familiar with Jewish customs and Judea's geography.

John 21:20, 24 state that "the disciple whom Jesus loved" wrote this Gospel, and John was one of Jesus' three closest disciples (Mark 9:2; 14:32–33).

The Muratorian Fragment, dated to AD 170, states that John's fellow disciples urged him to write a Gospel. John was at first hesitant, but eventually agreed to do so if they reviewed it. This is confirmed by the "we" in the following: "This is the disciple who testifies to these things and who wrote them down. We know that his testimony is true" (John 21:24 NIV).

44

Is Mark 16:9-20 the original
ending to the Gospel of Mark?

Mark 16:6–7 reports that after the women who had followed Jesus discovered the stone rolled away from His tomb, an angel told them that He had risen from the dead and to go tell His disciples. Then Mark 16:8 (NKJV) states, "So they went out quickly and fled from the tomb, for they trembled and were amazed. And they said nothing to anyone, for they were afraid."

And there, according to many scholars, the Gospel of Mark ends. In some Bible translations, such as the New International Version, the following note appears: "[The earliest manuscripts and some other ancient witnesses do not have verses 9–20.]" By "the earliest manuscripts," they mean the Codex Vaticanus and Codex Siniaticus, dated around AD 350. However, it seems highly unlikely that Mark would have deliberately ended his Gospel on such an abrupt note. On the other hand, verses 9–14 and 19–20 *do* read like a summary tacked on the end to bring a conclusion where one was lacking. Mary Magdalene is mentioned in verse 1, yet is *re*introduced in verse 9 with information that echoes Luke 8:2.

It is likely that Mark originally had a different ending but that it was lost—or possibly the end of the sheet of papyrus broke off. So an editor compiled information from other sources and penned a brief ending. Why not? We know that godly men were later inspired to add editorial notes to the Law of Moses, and we don't think anything amiss—so why should we find it disingenuous that a Christian editor should do the same?

The inspired editor clearly had access to original documents, as evidenced by the sayings of Jesus he quoted in Mark 16:15–18. This process was nothing new. For example, Luke did not write his Gospel by direct revelation; he composed it from already-existing material and eyewitness testimony, which he judiciously arranged and edited.

45
Why do some believe that the story of the woman caught in adultery should not be part of the Bible?

The story of the woman caught in adultery (also known as the *Pericope Adulterae*) is a well-known and much-loved passage found in our Bible translations today. It's so in keeping with the religious confrontations of Jesus' day, His forgiveness, and His command to lead a godly life that it's hard for many to believe that it wasn't originally part of John's Gospel. Yet for decades, Bible versions such as the NIV contained this disclaimer: "[The earliest manuscripts and many other ancient witnesses do not have John 7:53– 8:11.]"

The four earliest manuscripts, P66 and P75 (from the AD 200s) and Codex Siniaticus and Codex Vaticanus (from around AD 350), don't contain it—although they *do* contain diacritical (editorial) marks in their margins acknowledging the existence of the excluded story. However, the Didascalia (AD 230) mentions it, and Didymus the Blind (AD 313–398) reported that the story was found in several copies. Augustine (AD 354–430) argued that it was authentic but that it had been excluded by editors who feared that it gave women license to commit adultery.

So is this passage inspired scripture? The evangelical New Testament scholar Dr. Daniel B. Wallace, while researching New Testament manuscripts in Albania, found that the story was lacking in three of the texts, and was in an entirely different place in a fourth manuscript—at the *end* of John's Gospel. He therefore believes that it was *not* originally part of the biblical text.

Other scholars believe the story is scriptural. They reason that although it wasn't originally part of John's text, the early Church recognized it as an authentic story and therefore added it to his Gospel. They probably chose to add it at *this* spot because that's when the incident happened. Notice that a few verses later Jesus said, "I pass judgment on no one" (John 8:15 NIV).

46

How many differences are there between the various Greek manuscripts?

The two previous Q&A's refer to the largest and best-known differences in the ancient New Testament texts, but there are many thousands of minor variations (called "textual variants") in the Greek texts. This has caused some skeptics to assert that there are *so many* differences that we can never truly know what the *original* text actually said. But this is a deliberately exaggerated view, one the actual evidence does not warrant.

There are two reasons for the large number of textual variants. First, they not only include accidental omissions and additions, but also tiny variations in spelling or different arrangements of the same words, even though such differences almost never alter the meaning of the text. In other words, even the most insignificant differences count as variants—and the overwhelming majority of these differences *are* insignificant. They don't affect any important Christian doctrine.

Second, there are more than fifty-five hundred copies of Greek New Testament manuscripts in existence. (This doesn't even include ten thousand Latin manuscripts or five thousand manuscripts in other ancient languages.) While the majority of these Greek texts come from later centuries, about twelve come from the AD 100s, sixty-four date back to the AD 200s, and forty-eight copies were made in the AD 300s. Together, these early copies contain the complete New

Testament several times over. The New Testament is the best-attested book from the ancient world.

Can we be certain that the scriptures we have today are the same as the original New Testament? Yes, we can! After comparing the various copies, and by sifting out the countless insignificant variations, scholars (and we) have an excellent idea of what the original autographs of the New Testament really said.

47
Which Greek manuscripts are the most accurate New Testament texts?

First of all, it's important to know that most New Testament manuscripts belong to one of three textual "families." The differences between these textual groups cause both scholars and laypeople to advocate one above another. This dispute goes back sixteen hundred years.

For example, the Old Latin translations, including the Latin Vulgate, are based upon a text that has come to be called the Western Text. When Jerome produced the Vulgate around AD 400, he also had access to the Byzantine Text (of Lucian of Antioch) and the Alexandrian Text (of Hesychius of Egypt), but he spoke disparagingly of both. Thus, the Western Text, through Jerome's Latin translation, dominated Western Europe from about AD 400 until the 1500s.

During this same time, Christians of the Greek-speaking

Byzantine Empire continued using the Byzantine Text. After Constantinople fell in 1453, some of these manuscripts were brought to the West, where in 1515 a Dutch scholar named Erasmus compiled them into one text (later called the *Textus Receptus*—meaning "Received Text"). Martin Luther's New Testament and the King James Bible are based upon this text, and it dominated the Christian world for 450 years.

Then, in the 1800s, scholars discovered the *Codex Siniaticus*; plus the *Codex Vaticanus* was made public. Both copies were produced around AD 350 and mostly represent the Alexandrian Text. Once again, the "new" readings were compiled into one text, which scholars believed was the most accurate version. Most modern Bible translations are largely based on this text.

So which text is most accurate? While some people exclusively favor one text and speak disparagingly of all others, many scholars believe that *all* these texts have an important part to contribute. It's worth noting that there are far more differences in our modern Bibles due to translation styles than to differences in the original Greek texts.

48
How reliable are biblical accounts of Jesus' miracles?

One of the premises of what has come to be called "higher criticism" is that only the Bible's historical and plausible statements are to be accepted—and *then* only after being reinterpreted and adjusted. All miracles and supernatural events are automatically dismissed as later embellishments. In their search for the "real, historical Jesus," skeptics typically view the biblical texts as falsified and unreliable—except when a verse lines up with their views.

At least you have to give them credit for acknowledging that Jesus *existed*. Some decades ago, it was popular to state that the Church had invented myths about a man called Jesus. But the evidence of Jesus' existence, even in secular history, is too strong, and critics were eventually forced to bow to the facts. Today, no credible historian denies that Jesus lived.

As for miracles, if you believe that God created the world and that Jesus told the truth when He claimed to be God's Son, then certainly He had the power to do miracles—yes, even to raise the dead, calm a raging storm, and walk on the sea. Miracles often contradict the normal laws of nature, but that doesn't make them impossible. After all, God created the laws of nature in the first place, so He's able to supersede them when He desires. As Jesus said, "The things which are impossible with men are possible with God" (Luke 18:27 KJV).

Jesus did healing miracles because, in a day when

doctors were few and medicine rudimentary, the fact that He healed people showed that God loved them. His miracles also demonstrated God's power and proved that He was the Messiah (Luke 7:19–22). Jesus' many miracles finally culminated in His greatest miracle of all—when He rose from the dead. This, the apostle Paul wrote, was the definitive proof that Jesus was God's Son (Romans 1:3–4).

49
Did Jesus heal one blind man as He entered Jericho or two blind men as He left?

Jesus and His disciples, with a large crowd following them, were walking to Jerusalem when, near Jericho, two blind men heard the excitement and asked what was happening. When the crowd told them Jesus was passing through, the blind men cried out to Him to have mercy on them. The crowd sternly told them to be quiet, but they shouted even louder, so Jesus called them and asked what they wanted. When they replied that they wished to receive their sight, He immediately healed them.

The details in all three Synoptic Gospels correspond *so* closely that it's clear they're all referring to the same incident. However, there are differences.

Luke tells us, "As Jesus was approaching Jericho, a blind man was sitting by the road" (Luke 18:35 NASB). Matthew says, "As they were leaving Jericho. . .two blind men [were] sitting by the road" (Matthew 20:29–30 NASB). Mark agrees with Matthew that this happened "as He was leaving Jericho" but tells of only *one* blind man, named Bartimaeus (Mark 10:46–47 NASB).

As Matthew states, there were *two* blind men. But Mark focused only on Bartimaeus since he was the best-known of the two.

As for *where* this miracle happened, since most of the details are identical, it's unlikely that Jesus healed one blind man as He entered Jericho and two more as He left. The answer is found in the fact that the *old* city of Jericho was almost uninhabited in Jesus' day and that King Herod had built a *new* city of Jericho a mile to the south. Jesus and His disciples had apparently stopped at the old city to rest then continued on to the new city.

In Bible times, beggars normally sat just outside a city's gates. These blind men had wisely positioned themselves farther away, "by the road," so they could be first in line for travelers' charity.

50

Why do the Gospels give three different dates for Jesus driving the merchants from the temple?

Matthew tells us that after riding into Jerusalem in His Triumphal Entry, "Jesus entered the temple courts and drove out all who were buying and selling there. He overturned the tables of the money changers and the benches of those selling doves" (Matthew 21:12 NIV). Then He went to Bethany for the night. The next morning, as He returned to Jerusalem, He cursed a fig tree (Matthew 21:17–19). Luke agrees with Matthew's order of events (Luke 19:28–46).

Mark, however, tells us that after Jesus rode into Jerusalem and entered the temple area, He apparently just "looked around" before heading to Bethany. The next morning, He cursed the fig tree *then* cleansed the temple (Mark 11:1–17).

Now, John doesn't mention Jesus clearing out the temple in AD 30, but tells us He did so three years *earlier* (John 2:13–16). These are clear contradictions, aren't they?

No, they're not. Jesus cleared out the temple at least *twice*. On the first occasion, the Jews said that it had taken forty-six years to build the temple thus far (John 2:20 NIV). We know from secular history that Herod began to rebuild the temple around 20 BC. That makes the date of this first incident around AD 26 or 27, at the start of Jesus' earthly ministry.

As for the different days between Mark's account and Matthew's and Luke's, the most likely scenario is that Jesus cleansed the temple two days in a row. Remember, He'd done the exact same thing at a Passover three years earlier, and on that occasion He *first* braided a whip to drive them out. He obviously felt *very* strongly about what the merchants had been doing in the temple.

The other possibility is that Mark recorded the event out of order. "Mark. . .wrote down accurately whatsoever he remembered. It was not, however, in exact order that he related the sayings or deeds of Christ" (Eusebius, *Church History*, Book 3, Chapter 39:15).

51
Why do the Gospels give two different dates for the Passover supper?

The Synoptic Gospels declare that Jesus and His disciples ate the Last Supper on Thursday after sundown, which was the Passover (Matthew 26:17–19; Mark 14:12–17; Luke 22:7–15). Indeed, Jewish Christians point out that it has the earmarks of being a Passover meal.

But John *seems* to say that this meal was "before the Feast of the Passover" and was an ordinary evening meal (John 13:1–2 NKJV). He also states that when the Jewish leaders took Jesus to Pilate the next morning, that "to avoid ceremonial uncleanness they did not enter the palace, because they wanted to be able to eat the Passover" (John 18:28 NIV). Later, John tells us this day "was the day of Preparation of the Passover" (John 19:14 NIV).

In his book *The New Testament Documents*, F. F. Bruce argued that a majority of Jews, including Jesus and His disciples, may have celebrated Passover a day before the chief priests and their circle. Perhaps different people followed different calendars—one pre-Exilic and one post-Exilic. Also, there may have been a practical reason: The priests may have simply been too exhausted from slaughtering thousands of lambs to observe Passover that day.

If, however, there was only *one* Passover meal, then when John says it was "just before the Passover Festival," he means the festival began with *that* meal. Even though the priests ate Passover that evening, they didn't want to be ritually defiled the next morning because there were a *series* of meals during the Passover Festival—the weeklong Feast of Unleavened Bread. Also, "the day of Preparation" means Friday, the day before the Sabbath, so the "day of Preparation of the Passover" was the Friday during Passover week. This was also why that Saturday was "a special Sabbath" (John 19:14, 31 NIV).

52
Why do the four Gospels give conflicting accounts of Peter denying Jesus?

At a casual glance, there appear to be contradictions between the Gospels regarding the details of Peter denying Jesus. But this is resolved if you look at all four Gospel accounts of this event side-by-side. Now, it should be pointed out that Matthew 26:57–75 and Mark 14:53–72 agree *very* closely. Not only do they tell the events in the same order, but their wording is almost identical.

Luke recounts the same details but in different order. Instead of describing Peter entering Caiaphas's courtyard, then the high priest interrogating Jesus, then refocusing on Peter, Luke tells Peter's story all together (Luke 22:54–62), *then* talks about Christ's appearance before Caiaphas (22:63–71). The events in the courtyard were happening at the same time as the events in Caiaphas's chamber, so it's valid to present them either way. Amazingly enough, despite Luke's different arrangement, his text is virtually identical.

John 18:12–27, however, adds new details. John tells us that the mob *first* took Jesus to Annas, Caiaphas's father-in-law. John knew this because he was there and was the one who got Peter into Annas's courtyard. John had firsthand information about Annas questioning Jesus, so *that's* what he writes about, while saying nothing about the interrogation at Caiaphas's house. Apparently, after Peter mingled with the servants in Annas's courtyard, he traveled with them when they took Jesus to Caiaphas's house.

When you read only Matthew, Mark, and Luke (which don't mention the stop at Annas's house), you might come to the conclusion that all three denials took place at Caiaphas's house. But John reveals that Peter first denied Jesus in Annas's courtyard then did so a second and third time in Caiaphas's courtyard. Another equally plausible interpretation, however, is that Peter denied Jesus *once* at Annas's house and then another *three* times at Caiaphas's house.

53
Were all Jews cursed for all time for crucifying Jesus?

Not all Jewish people were brought under a curse for crucifying Christ, even though a mob in Pilate's courtyard cried out, "His blood be on us, and on our children" (Matthew 27:25 KJV).

Who, then, was responsible for crucifying Jesus? The Bible says "the chief priests, the scribes, and the elders of the people assembled at the palace of the high priest, who was called Caiaphas, and plotted to take Jesus by trickery and kill Him. But they said, 'Not during the feast, lest there be an uproar among the people'" (Matthew 26:3–5 NKJV).

Scripture also tells us that "They wanted to arrest him, but they were afraid of the crowds" (Matthew 21:46 NLT). The common Jewish people loved Jesus and "heard him gladly" (Mark 12:37 KJV). They were the "great multitude" who cheered when He rode into Jerusalem (John 12:12). Had the chief priests tried to arrest Jesus publicly, the people would have rioted. A multitude of such Jews became believers after Jesus rose from the dead (Acts 2:41; 4:4).

The Bible states that it was the small group of corrupt leaders—"the chief priests, the scribes, and the elders"—who plotted to kill Jesus (see Matthew 26:14, 47, 57, 59; 27:1–2; John 7:31–32). Jesus Himself had prophesied that He would die at the hands of the religious rulers (Matthew 16:21). These leaders sent a mob of zealous followers to arrest Jesus, and it was this crowd that filled Pilate's courtyard a few hours later, obeyed the rulers' orders, and called down a curse upon themselves (Matthew 26:47; 27:20, 24–25).

This curse was *not* brought upon the heads of *all* Jews, nor for *all time*. It was fulfilled in Jesus' enemies and their (then-grown) children forty years later in AD 70, when Roman legions besieged Jerusalem and slew those who had been fighting against them.

54
How should Christians respond to charges that the New Testament is anti-Semitic?

Neither the Gospels nor the book of Acts nor the epistles of Paul are anti-Semitic. Sadly, however, it's true that some bigoted people down through the centuries have quoted them out of context to help incite hatred and pogroms against the Jewish people.

For example, Jesus said to certain Jews, "You are of your father the devil" (John 8:44 NKJV), but it's vital to remember that He was not speaking to *all* Jews, only to those who hated Him and were plotting to kill Him (8:37–40). Also, Jesus' scathing rebuke in Matthew 23 was directed at the hypocritical religious *leaders*, not the poor and vulnerable Jewish people those leaders were oppressing.

Six hundred years earlier, the prophet Jeremiah spoke out so sharply against the sins of his people that the rulers and priests denounced him as a false prophet, labeled him the enemy of the people, and threw him into prison (Jeremiah 28:5–11; 37:11–15; 38:1–4). Yet, within seventy years, the Jews realized that Jeremiah had been right and counted him among the greatest of their prophets. At times, Jesus' messages were so akin to Jeremiah's that many Jews thought He was Jeremiah come back to life (Matthew 16:13–14). Both Jeremiah and Jesus loved and wept over those who had rejected them (Lamentations 1:15–16; Luke 19:41–44).

The book of Acts records how certain Jews persecuted

Christians, and the apostle Paul had strong words for such men, but he talked about Gentile persecutors in the same breath (1 Thessalonians 2:14–16). Paul, who had great love for his fellow Jews, wrote, "I have great sorrow and continual grief in my heart" for them and "my heart's desire and prayer to God for Israel is that they may be saved" (Romans 9:2; 10:1 NKJV). Like Jeremiah and Jesus, Paul wept for his people.

55
How could the New Testament writers recite conversations they hadn't even heard?

We can easily understand how the apostles could have written about things they'd personally seen and heard. But the New Testament also quotes a number of private conversations between the ruling authorities and religious leaders.

For example, Matthew 14:1–12 tells us about King Herod Antipas's private dealings with and statements about John the Baptist, and Mark 6:14 relates Herod's musings about Jesus. How did the disciples learn these details? The answer can be found in scripture.

Luke 8:3 reports that Joanna (the wife of Chuza, King Herod's steward) was one of Jesus' close disciples. Luke also tells us that there was a prominent disciple in the early Church named Manaen "who had been brought up with Herod the tetrarch" (Acts 13:1 NIV). Both of these people were likely excellent inside sources for the apostles.

But what about the following? Matthew 26:14–16 and 27:3–7 tell of Judas's private conversations with the chief priests; Matthew 28:2 4, 11–15 relates the conspiracy be-tween the chief priests and the guards to deny Jesus' resur-rection; Acts 4:13–17 specifically states that the religious leaders put the disciples out of the room before they held their council and did the same thing in Acts 5:29–39. So how were the Gospel writers able to recount what their enemies had conspired to do when their plans were made behind closed doors?

Again, they had inside contacts. Both Nicodemus and Joseph of Arimathea were members of the Sanhedrin, the Jewish ruling council, yet were secret disciples of Jesus (Mark 15:43; John 3:1–2). Also, a number of lower-level priests who initially went along with the plots against Jesus became so upset with the cover-up and deception that they became Christians; in fact, "a great company of the priests were obedient to the faith" (Acts 6:7 KJV). Apparently, when they became believers, they passed along what they'd seen and heard.

56

How did Judas die— by hanging himself or by falling and bursting open?

═══════════════════

At first read, there appears to be a contradiction between the accounts of Judas's death recorded in the Bible.

Matthew tells us that after Judas betrayed Jesus for thirty pieces of silver, "he threw down the pieces of silver in the temple and departed, and went and hanged himself. But the chief priests took the silver pieces and. . .bought with them the potter's field, to bury strangers in. Therefore that field has been called the Field of Blood to this day" (Matthew 27:5–8 NKJV).

Luke tells us, "With the payment he received for his wickedness, Judas bought a field; there he fell headlong, his body burst open and all his intestines spilled out. Everyone in Jerusalem heard about this, so they called that field in their language Akeldama, that is, Field of Blood" (Acts 1:18–19 NIV).

Luke doesn't contradict Matthew, however. Rather, he adds new details that give a fuller picture of Judas's death. The Potter's Field was located south of Jerusalem in the Valley of Hinnom and was known for its rich clay, which the locals used for making pottery. Judas hanged himself there. Apparently, his body wasn't discovered for a few days, and decomposition was well under way. When someone discovered the body and cut the rope, Judas' body hit the ground, burst, and his intestines spilled out.

With the potter's field now defiled, potters could no longer use its clay. No one would have bought their wares. The priests probably reminded the owners of this fact and then offered to buy the land with Judas's money. As far as Christians were concerned, it was called the Field of Blood because the money had been paid to betray Jesus' "innocent blood" (Matthew 27:4). However, the story of Judas's death and bloody fall was widely known in Jerusalem, and *they* considered it the Field of Blood for that reason.

57
Why does Matthew say Jeremiah gave a prophecy that Zechariah actually gave?

After Judas betrayed Jesus, he rushed back to the temple, threw down the thirty pieces of silver he'd received for his betrayal, and left. The priests then bought the potter's field with his money.

Matthew wrote that this event fulfilled a 550-year-old prophecy: "Then was fulfilled what was spoken by Jeremiah the prophet, saying, 'And they took the thirty pieces of silver, the value of Him who was priced, whom they of the children of Israel priced, and gave them for the potter's field, as the LORD directed me'" (Matthew 27:9–10 NKJV).

This is an amazingly fulfilled prophecy; however, Zechariah, not Jeremiah, was the one who delivered it: "So they weighed out for my wages thirty pieces of silver. And the LORD said to me, 'Throw it to the potter'—that princely price they set on me. So I took the thirty pieces of silver and threw them into the house of the LORD for the potter" (Zechariah 11:12–13 NKJV).

But these events *were* also foreshadowed in the book of Jeremiah. God told Jeremiah to take elders and priests into the same Valley of Hinnom (Tophet), hurl a potter's vessel on the ground, and prophesy, "Thus says the LORD of hosts: 'Even so I will break this people and this city, as one breaks a potter's vessel. . .and they shall bury them in Tophet'" (Jeremiah 19:11 NKJV).

Judas fell and broke open like the potter's vessel. And just as priests went to the valley with Jeremiah, six hundred years later priests went there to buy a field to "bury them in Tophet." Even Judas's lament, "I have betrayed innocent blood" (Matthew 27:4 NIV) is seen in Jeremiah's declaration that they were guilty of "the blood of the innocent" (Jeremiah 19:4 NIV).

Matthew was referring to prophetic imagery in the books of Jeremiah *and* Zechariah and, as was sometimes done, cited only the *major* prophet (compare Mark 1:2–3 with Isaiah 40:3 and Malachi 3:1).

58
What did the writing above Jesus' cross actually say?

In Roman times, when a criminal was sentenced to be crucified, it was customary to write the charges against him on a small board, called in Latin a *titulus*. Someone carried this board in front of the condemned man as he bore his cross to the place of execution. One of the man's executioners then nailed the board to the cross above the crucified man's head.

Matthew tells us that the charge affixed to the top of Jesus' cross read, "This is Jesus the King of the Jews" (Matthew 27:37 NLT). Mark tells us that it read simply, "The King of the Jews" (Mark 15:26 NLT). Luke tells us that the writing said, "This is the King of the Jews" (Luke 23:38 NLT). And finally, John tells us that the writing said, "Jesus of Nazareth, the King of the Jews" (John 19:19 NLT).

While the meaning of all four phrases is the same, why are there differences? The answer is found in John 19:20 (NKJV), which states that "it was written in Hebrew, Greek, and Latin." The wording in each of these three languages was slightly different.

In Latin, John's title reads *Iesus Nazarenus Rex Iudaeorum*, and from an early date Latin Christians used the initials *INRI* as a symbol of Christ. Now, John's text is the only one that mentions Nazareth (hence the "N"), plus he's the only one who refers to the charge as a "title" (Latin *titulus*), so John quoted the Latin reading.

Matthew (writing for the Jews) quoted the Hebrew

wording, and Luke (writing for the Greeks) quoted the Greek wording. In all cases, the core of the accusation was, "The King of the Jews," so Mark (known for his brief style) simply stated that. Jesus' enemies wanted this accusation changed to read, "He said, 'I am the King of the Jews,'" but Pilate refused (John 19:21–22 NKJV).

59
Why do the Gospel writers often relate the same incident differently?

Although Matthew, Mark, and Luke all drew their stories about Jesus from a common source, each one was inspired to select stories and edit them according to the needs of their audiences. Matthew wrote to convince the Jews that Jesus was the Messiah. Luke, writing for the Greeks, was often led to choose different stories, and even when he related the *same* events, he frequently related different aspects of them.

For example, in the final moments before Jesus died on the cross, Matthew records Him saying, "My God, my God, why have you forsaken me?" (Matthew 27:46 NIV). Later, Matthew tells us Jesus cried out with a loud voice and died—but doesn't tell us His final words (verse 50). Luke, for his part, *doesn't* record Jesus asking why God had forsaken Him. Instead he tells us, "Jesus called out with a loud voice, 'Father, into your hands I commit my spirit.' When he had said this, he breathed his last" (Luke 23:46 NIV).

Matthew chose the saying he did because it was a direct quote from Psalm 22:1. In Psalm 22 David prophesied with chilling accuracy about the crucifixion of Israel's Messiah (see verses 14–18). Luke's Greek audience didn't have a background in the Jewish scriptures, so this quote would have meant nothing to them—and would have just confused them. They did, however, have a strong philosophical belief that a god (or divine man) would act calmly in the face of tragedy. Luke selected his quote with that in mind.

Jesus *did* utter both declarations, and since Luke was writing a new Gospel—and not simply copying Matthew's Gospel word for word—he chose different details to reach his readers. Christians believe this was not simply an editorial decision but that God inspired him in this.

60

How do we know Jesus actually died on the cross? Isn't it possible He just fell unconscious and later revived in the cool tomb?

People who don't want to believe that Jesus rose from the dead have come up with several theories stating that He never died in the first place and that He may have just *appeared* to resurrect. One of the most persistent (but pathetic) hypotheses is the Swoon Theory, which holds that Jesus just fainted from pain and exhaustion and only *appeared* dead. Roman soldiers then allowed Him to be taken down from the cross and placed in the tomb, where He revived. A variation of this theory states that the vinegar Jesus sipped (John 19:28–30) was actually a drug that induced a temporary comatose state.

However, falling unconscious would have caused Jesus to die within minutes. A well-known aspect of crucifixion is that the victim had to continually push himself up with his legs in order to breathe. Remaining hanging in a slumped position caused quick asphyxiation.

In addition, to make *sure* Jesus was dead, a Roman soldier pierced His side with a spear, impaling His heart, and causing blood to gush out (John 19:31–37).

Other conspiracy theorists doubt that Jesus died after hanging on the cross for only six hours, since it normally took two to four days for the victim of crucifixion to die. Pilate himself was surprised that Jesus expired so quickly

(Mark 15:44). Medical authorities, however, point out that when Jesus was whipped with a flagellum, the many deep cuts caused considerable blood loss and induced hypovolemic shock. Jesus had been so weakened by the ordeal that He was unable to carry His crossbar to Golgotha (Matthew 27:26, 32).

Even skeptics admit that *had* Jesus somehow (barely) survived His crucifixion, He'd have been so weakened and pitiful that He could hardly have presented Himself as the Lord of Life.

There can be no doubt that Jesus was dead when He was taken down from the cross—or that God raised Him from the dead three days later.

61

How do we know Jesus' disciples didn't steal His body from the tomb and falsely claim He had been raised from the dead?

Another argument against Jesus' literal resurrection is the theory that His disciples stole His body from the tomb so that they could claim that He had been raised from the dead in fulfillment of Old Testament prophecies about the Messiah. After all, skeptics point out, Jesus *had* repeatedly told His disciples He'd be killed and then rise again (Matthew 16:21; 17:22–23; 20:17–19). Even Jesus' enemies were aware of this prophecy (Matthew 27:62–63).

However, *because* the chief priests were worried that someone could steal the body, they assigned several soldiers (whether Roman soldiers or Jewish Temple guards) to stand watch at Jesus' tomb. When this failed to stop Jesus from rising, the priests went into "damage control" mode and started a rumor that Jesus' disciples had stolen His body (Matthew 27:62–66; 28:1–4, 11–15).

Also, even though Jesus had repeatedly talked about it, the disciples didn't know "what the rising from the dead meant" (Mark 9:9–10 NKJV). Plus "they did not know the Scripture, that He must rise again from the dead" (John 20:9 NKJV). Only later did Jesus explain *which* Old Testament scriptures His resurrection had fulfilled (Luke 24:27; Acts 2:24–31).

Plus, the mob that arrested Jesus had so terrified His disciples that they scattered into the night. Even after news of His resurrection reached them, they remained huddled in a house with the door locked, for fear of their enemies (Mark 14:43, 50; John 20:19).

Very importantly, stealing Jesus' body then publicly proclaiming what they *knew* to be a *lie* would have gone against everything Jesus stood for and had taught the disciples. It also contradicts the proclamations in the book of Acts that the disciples believed Jesus *had* resurrected and were willing to suffer martyrdom for that belief.

Finally, such a scenario doesn't explain how the disciples saw Jesus after His resurrection (1 Corinthians 15:3–8).

62

Weren't Jesus' disciples suffering hallucinations when they "saw" Him again?

Some have held that it is possible that the disciples experienced emotion-induced hallucinations when they saw Jesus after His death. However, while individuals may hallucinate, a crowd doesn't see such shared visions. But that's exactly what the *disciples* themselves thought at first.

When the women who followed Jesus reported that they'd seen Him, the men thought they'd been seeing things and "they did not believe the women, because their words seemed to them like nonsense" (Luke 24:11 NIV).

The disciples' opinion about what the women had really seen changed immediately when Jesus entered the room and ten of *them* saw Him. They knew they were not having hallucinations but "were startled and frightened, thinking they saw a ghost" (Luke 24:37 NIV).

Jesus immediately set them straight. He said, "Why are your hearts filled with doubt? Look at my hands. Look at my feet. You can see that it's really me. Touch me and make sure that I am not a ghost, because ghosts don't have bodies, as you see that I do" (Luke 24:38–39 NLT). He commanded them to touch Him and they surely did. Within *one* minute, Jesus was upgraded in their minds from a hallucination to a ghost to solid reality.

To further prove He was really alive, Jesus asked for some food. "So they gave Him a piece of a broiled fish and some honeycomb. And He took it and ate in their presence" (Luke 24:42–43 NKJV). The disciples also ate and drank *with* Jesus on other occasions (Acts 10:39–41).

Thomas wasn't there that first time Jesus appeared to the other ten remaining disciples. Seeing Jesus and even touching Him wasn't enough to convince him. He insisted he'd have to stick his finger in Jesus' wounds before he'd believe. And Jesus gave him that opportunity (John 20:24–28).

Yes, Jesus really rose from the dead, and He "presented Himself alive after His suffering by many infallible proofs" (Acts 1:3 NKJV).

63

How can apparent contradictions in the Gospel accounts of what happened that first Easter Sunday morning be explained?

People are often baffled by the differences in the four Gospels' details of the events surrounding Jesus' resurrection. Each Gospel recounts different combinations of women coming to His tomb and vary as to what they saw and heard. Some assume that the Gospels contradict one another so much that each invalidates the others' testimony.

This is evidence, however, that the Gospel writers are truthful, since witnesses who conspire to lie are very careful to make their stories line up—even in the tiniest details. In a court of law, superficial differences between testimonies actually render witnesses more credible.

Also, the differing Gospel reports of this event *can* be harmonized. All four accounts have been contracted into brief narratives, with all the women named together—yet there were almost certainly two groups of women who set out that morning from separate locations at different times. Mary Magdalene led one of those groups (John 20:1), and Susana, Salome, or Joanna—all prominent female disciples— led the other (Luke 8:1–3; 24:10; Mark 16:1).

It also helps clarify the order of events if you bear in mind that Mary Magdalene told Peter and John the news first, then *later* told the main group of apostles. John owned a house nearby, in Jerusalem, and he and Peter were there that morning (John 18:15–16; 19:26–27; 20:1–3). The other disciples, except for Thomas, had apparently retreated to Bethany, two miles distant, where they had previously stayed (Matthew 21:17; 26:56; John 20:24). So Mary and the women reported to two different groups in succession.

Also, the tomb was near the city (John 19:20, 41), so it didn't take long to travel there and back. Mary Magdalene is known to have visited the tomb twice (John 20:1–11) and probably went back a third time with the other Mary (Matthew 28:9–10).

64
Why do Stephen's statements about Abraham contradict what Genesis says?

In the New Testament, Stephen said, "The God of glory appeared to our father Abraham [Abram] when he was in Mesopotamia, before he dwelt in Haran, and said to him, 'Get out of your country and from your relatives, and come to a land that I will show you.' Then he came out of the land of the Chaldeans and dwelt in Haran. And from there, when his father was dead, He moved him to this land" (Acts 7:2–4 NKJV).

Yet Genesis 11:31 seems to say that *first* Abraham's father Terah took his family, including Abraham, from Ur of the Chaldeans to Haran. *Then* Genesis 12:1–5 says that God called Abraham from Haran into Canaan. So which account is right?

Genesis 12:1 *doesn't* say, "Then the LORD said to Abram: 'Get out of your country. . . .' " Rather, it says, "Now the LORD *had* said to Abram: 'Get out of your country. . . .' " (Genesis 12:1–2 NKJV). In other words, God had *already* spoken to Abraham back in Ur.

But this still leaves another question: Genesis 11:26 (NKJV) says, "Terah lived seventy years, and begot Abram, Nahor, and Haran." Then verse 32 says that Terah died in Haran at 205 years of age. But both Genesis and Acts say that Abraham left Haran *after* his father died. Yet Genesis 12:4 says that Abraham was seventy-five years old when he left Haran, and 70 + 75 = 145, not 205. Did Terah live another sixty years after Abraham left Haran?

No. The answer is that Abram, Nahor, and Haran weren't triplets but were born in separate years. One son was born when their father was seventy, another some years after, and Abraham was born sixty years after the firstborn son—quite possibly from a second wife. Abraham was mentioned first simply because he was the most notable son.

65
Why did Stephen say
seventy-five of Jacob's descendants
went to Egypt when only seventy did?

Stephen said, "Joseph sent for his father Jacob and his whole family, seventy-five in all" (Acts 7:14 NIV). Yet Genesis says, "With the two sons who had been born to Joseph in Egypt, the members of Jacob's family, which went to Egypt, were seventy in all" (Genesis 46:27 NIV).

How did Stephen come up with seventy-five? Well, since he was a Hellenistic Jew (one who spoke and read Greek, not Hebrew), he quoted from the Greek translation of the Old Testament, the Septuagint. In this translation, Genesis 46:27 says: "And the sons of Joseph, who were born to him in the land of Egypt, were nine souls; all the souls of the house of Jacob who came with Joseph into Egypt, were seventy-five souls" (translated by Sir L. C. L. Brenton, 1851).

In this instance, the Septuagint gives a fuller number

than the Masoretic text, listing nine sons of Joseph, not just his first two. Joseph was the *last* of his brothers to get married, and he had only two sons when Jacob came to Egypt (Genesis 48:5–6)—but Joseph had seven more sons after that.

When you subtract Er and Onan, who died in Canaan, and Ephraim and Manasseh, who were born in Egypt, you have this equation: 70 – 4 = 66. That's why Genesis 46:26 (NKJV) specifies: "All the persons who went with Jacob to Egypt. . .were sixty-six persons in all." Thus, 66 + Joseph's 9 = 75.

Note: these seventy-five people were Jacob's sons and grandsons—not his daughters and granddaughters. At that time, women weren't named in genealogical lists. Dinah was an exception (Genesis 46:15). But Jacob's sons had wives, and Jacob likely had as many daughters as sons. (These unnamed daughters are mentioned in Genesis 37:34–35.) So the *total* number of Jacob's family who came down into Egypt was probably close to 150.

66

Who bought the field in Shechem— Jacob or Abraham?

Stephen said, "Jacob went down to Egypt and there he and our fathers died. From there they were removed to Shechem and laid in the tomb which Abraham had purchased for a sum of money from the sons of Hamor in Shechem" (Acts 7:15–16 NASB).

When Jacob returned to Canaan, *he* bought a field from "the sons of Hamor" (Amorites) in Shechem (Genesis 33:18–20). Abraham, however, had purchased a field with a cave-tomb from "the sons of Heth" (Hittites) at Hebron (Genesis 23). He was buried there, as were Isaac and Jacob (Genesis 25:7–10; 49:29–33; 50:12–13).

Joseph was entombed at Shechem (Joshua 24:32), and it appears from Acts 7 that his brothers were also. But the question is: If Abraham bought land in Hebron but *not* in Shechem, did Stephen get his facts mixed up?

Bible commentators point out that it was common practice for Jews to contract long, complex narratives into brief statements, so they'd have understood Stephen doing that—even if it seems odd to us today.

However, consider that 205 years before Jacob bought a field and erected an altar by "the" terebinth tree of Shechem (Genesis 33:18–20; 35:4), Abraham entered Canaan and stopped at Shechem, where he *also* built an altar by "the" famous terebinth tree (Genesis 12:5–7). Now, did Abraham build his altar then abandon it? The spot was sacred to him.

God had appeared there and promised, "To your descendants I will give this land" (Genesis 12:7 NKJV). Abraham likely bought the field with the nearby hillside to ensure that his altar remained standing after he moved.

But after a 205-year absence, the Amorites likely reclaimed the land. So Jacob, desiring to reconfirm the promise made to *him* (Abraham's "descendant"), was constrained to buy it again. Then he rebuilt the altar.

67

What exactly did the men traveling to Damascus with Saul (Paul) hear. . .or *not* hear?

Around AD 35, Paul (then called Saul) was traveling to Damascus to persecute Christians. One account says, "As he journeyed. . .suddenly a light shone around him from heaven. Then he fell to the ground, and heard a voice saying to him, 'Saul, Saul, why are you persecuting Me?'" (Acts 9:3–4 NKJV). This was Jesus speaking. Verse 7 adds, "And the men who journeyed with him stood speechless, hearing a voice but seeing no one."

Yet when Paul spoke to a crowd in Jerusalem some twenty years later, he said, "And those who were with me indeed saw the light and were afraid, but they did not hear the voice of Him who spoke to me" (Acts 22:9 NKJV).

First we are told that Paul's companions heard a voice, but then Paul says they didn't hear a voice. Which one is correct?

They both are. The Greek word *phone*, translated as "voice," means both "voice" and "sound." Thus the New International Version says: "The men traveling with Saul. . . heard the sound but did not see anyone" (Acts 9:7 NIV), and has Paul stating that his fellow travelers "did not understand the voice of him who was speaking to me" (Acts 22:9 NIV).

Paul saw and heard Jesus (1 Corinthians 15:8), but his companions weren't spiritually attuned. They saw the light but couldn't make out Jesus' form; they heard a sound but couldn't understand the words—and possibly weren't even sure it was a voice.

A similar thing had happened before in scripture. Jesus prayed, " 'Father, glorify Your name.' Then a voice came out of heaven: 'I have both glorified it, and will glorify it again.' So the crowd of people who stood by and heard it were saying that it had thundered; others were saying, 'An angel has spoken to Him' " (John 12:28–29 NASB; see also Daniel 10:7).

68

Why weren't Paul's pastoral epistles part of the first Bible canon?

Paul wrote ten of his thirteen epistles between AD 51 and his release from house arrest in Rome in AD 62. After that, he wrote his final letters, called pastoral epistles. They were 1 Timothy and Titus (written AD 63–65) and 2 Timothy (written during his final Roman imprisonment in around AD 67–68).

When the heretic Marcion compiled his canon in AD 144, he included Paul's first ten epistles, but not the final three. This has led some critics to question whether the pastoral epistles even existed by then—or if someone else (using Paul's name) wrote them later on.

Also, these three letters contain words and phrases Paul never used in his other epistles. For example, the expression "a trustworthy saying" appears five times in the pastoral epistles, but nowhere else in Paul's epistles. The words *godly* and *godliness* appear ten times in these epistles, but nowhere in Paul's letters. Based on these and other stylistic differences, many skeptics believe these epistles were later forgeries written in Paul's name.

However, the overall evidence is strong that Paul indeed wrote these epistles. The differences in vocabulary and word usage can be sufficiently explained by (a) Paul's recent experiences (he had been to Spain and back), (b) his immersion in the Latin West, and (c) the passage of several years. The early Church never doubted that Paul had written these three epistles. In fact, in the AD 170 Muratorian Fragment, an official Church list of Bible books, all three are mentioned as part of the New Testament canon.

As for why Marcion included only Paul's ten early epistles, it's likely that these epistles were compiled into one scroll for posterity during Paul's first imprisonment in AD 61–62, when it wasn't certain he'd be released. They would have circulated as one unit before the later three epistles were added. Marcion likely had access to the earlier compilation.

69
Did Paul and James disagree on the roles of grace and works for salvation?

The apostle Paul taught: "For it is by grace you have been saved, through faith—and this is not from yourselves, it is the gift of God—not by works" (Ephesians 2:8–9 NIV). However, many people assume that the apostle James's basic message is summed up by *this* verse: "You see then that a man is justified by works, and not by faith only" (James 2:24 NKJV).

It is simplistic to pit these verses against each other as if they represent conflicting views. Paul held that we're saved by grace and not by works, but he agreed with James's position (James 2:14–17) that mere mental assent to faith in Jesus won't save a person whose actions shout the opposite. Paul also warned against those who *professed* to know God "but in works they deny Him" (Titus 1:16 NKJV).

Doing good works won't save you, but Jesus taught that the fruit your life bears is the surest proof of who you really are (Matthew 7:20). This is why Paul stressed that "those who have believed in God should be careful to maintain good works" (Titus 3:8 NKJV)—not to keep yourself saved, but because God inspires you to do good works.

So did Paul and James believe the same thing? Yes, and this issue was settled back in AD 50. Some Christian Pharisees had argued that Jews and Gentiles alike had to obey the Law of Moses to be saved (Acts 15:1, 5). However, in a meeting under the leadership of Peter *and* James, Peter summed up the Jerusalem church's position when he stated, "We believe that we are all saved the same way, by the undeserved grace of the Lord Jesus" (Acts 15:11 NLT). Notice the "we."

This was James's position as well—that both Jews and Gentiles were saved not by good works but by *undeserved grace*.

70

Why are the words sometimes different when New Testament writers quote Old Testament passages?

The writers of the New Testament frequently quoted the Jewish scriptures (the Old Testament) to show how they were fulfilled in Christ. The wording of the quoted passages is often exactly the same as what we read in the present-day Old Testament, which is based upon the Masoretic Text. However, there are sometimes differences. For example, notice the variation between Psalm 40:6 and Hebrews 10:5.

Why the differences? Well, in the centuries before Christ, millions of Jews throughout the Greek-speaking world no longer spoke or read Hebrew, so in 285–250 BC Jewish scholars began translating the Hebrew scriptures into Greek. This translation, called the Septuagint—Latin for *seventy* (seventy translators, though one legend holds that there were seventy-two)—was completed in 132 BC. For centuries, this was most Jewish people's official version of the scriptures. Paul and other New Testament writers often quoted from this Greek translation.

So when there are differences between the Masoretic Text and the Septuagint, which is right? Many Christians believe that since the Septuagint was translated 285–132 BC, it was based on an earlier and more accurate Hebrew reading than the later Masoretic Text. They give a number of examples to support this view.

Here's one: Psalm 22 prophetically describes Jesus'

crucifixion. In the Septuagint, verse 16 says "They have pierced my hands and feet." But in the present-day Masoretic text, the same verse reads, "Like a lion are my hands and feet." Which reading is correct? Is the Hebrew word *k'aru* (pierced) the original reading, or is *k'ari* (like a lion)? In the two-thousand-year-old *Psalms Scroll*, written in Hebrew and found at Nahal Hever, Psalm 22:16 agrees with the Septuagint.

The Septuagint isn't *always* more accurate than the Masoretic Text (since not all of its books were translated with the same precision), but in many places it is.

71

When did Christians realize that the letters of the New Testament were also scripture?

Christians recognized most books of the New Testament as scripture very early on. This was because Jesus was the Messiah, the Son of God who had resurrected from the dead, who fulfilled the Old Testament scriptures and ushered in a new era. Therefore, the story and words of Jesus—and the written versions of the Gospels—were accepted as equal to the Old Testament scriptures.

In AD 63–65, Paul put the written sayings of Jesus on the same level as the Law of Moses. He wrote, "For the Scripture says, 'You shall not muzzle an ox while it treads out the grain,' and 'The laborer is worthy of his wages'" (1 Timothy 5:18 NKJV). The first passage Paul quoted was Deuteronomy 25:4, and the second passage was Luke 10:7.

In addition, early Christians recognized that the Holy Spirit had inspired the apostles. Paul wrote, "If anyone thinks himself to be a prophet or spiritual, let him acknowledge that the things which I write to you are the commandments of the Lord" (1 Corinthians 14:37 NKJV).

The apostle Peter acknowledged this very thing. As mentioned in a previous Q&A, most of Paul's letters had been circulating together since about AD 62. We know Peter had studied them, because he wrote in AD 65–68, "This is what our beloved brother Paul also wrote to you with the wisdom God gave him—speaking of all these things in all of his letters. . . . And those who are ignorant and unstable have twisted his letters to mean something quite different, just as they do with other parts of Scripture" (2 Peter 3:15–16 NLT).

It took longer for other books—Revelation, for example—to be accepted, but the Church acknowledged the bulk of the New Testament as canonical and as Scripture by AD 68.

72

Why did it take Christians over three hundred years to agree on which books belonged in the New Testament?

The Synoptic Gospels (Matthew, Mark, and Luke) were acknowledged as Scripture in AD 63–65, and Paul's first ten epistles were accepted by AD 68. John completed his Gospel around AD 90, and it was almost immediately accepted as canonical. Soon, the Church accepted 1 and 2 Timothy, Titus, Hebrews, 1 John, and 1 Peter.

In his writings, the Church father Irenaeus (AD 130–200) quoted from twenty-three of our twenty-seven New Testament books, and the Muratorian list shows that the church in Rome accepted the book of Revelation before AD 170. Virtually all the current New Testament books had been accepted by that date. But why weren't *all* Christians in agreement until AD 367?

In *Ecclesiastical History*, written in AD 300, Eusebius listed the "Recognized Books," then said, "Those that are disputed, yet familiar to most, include the epistles known as James, Jude, and 2 Peter, and those called 2 and 3 John." As for Revelation, he wrote that "some reject it, others include it among the Recognized Books" (Eusebius, *Ecclesiastical History*, Book 3, Chapter 25).

One of the reasons for slow universal acceptance of all these books was that the apostles Paul, Peter, and John were no longer around to pass judgment on them. Plus, communication was slow and more difficult back then, and epistles like James—written in Judea for Jewish Christians—weren't widely known in the Church at large. The Church fathers also exercised great caution before officially accepting an epistle as scripture.

In AD 367, Athanasius, Bishop of Alexandria, listed the same New Testament books we have today. However, he was not making a *decision* as to which books were scripture but merely reminding his readers what the Church had already acknowledged.

73
Did Constantine and the Roman Empire doctor the New Testament manuscripts?

Some Bible critics argue that after Constantine accepted Christianity, the Roman Empire took control of the Bible and then "doctored" it. In other words, there was a deliberate conspiracy to change the Bible text. The Romans' motive, the detractors say, was to better control the people.

However, there's absolutely no evidence that the Roman Empire changed the scriptures. In fact, when they are asked *which* parts of the text the Romans changed, most critics are at a loss for words. A logical assumption is that the Romans would have *added* passages like Romans 13:1–7, which commands Christians to be subject to the government, to not resist those in authority, to pay taxes, and to consider the authorities "God's ministers." Presumably, they would *also* have added 1 Peter 2:13–17 (or beefed it up if it existed), which admonishes Christians to submit to *every* law of man, and to "honor the king [Caesar]."

The problem with this theory, however, is that the Bible as we have it today can be checked against *earlier* copies of the scriptures. Constantine became a Christian in AD 312 and in AD 331 ordered Eusebius to provide fifty Bibles for churches. However, copies of the scriptures exist from *before* these dates. The Beatty Papyrus P46 contains Romans 13, which is identical to the text we have today. Scholars date it to AD 175–225—*at least* eighty years before Constantine became a Christian. As for Peter's commands, the Bodmer

Papyrus P72 contains the entire book of 1 Peter—including the passage 2:13–17. This document dates to AD 200, some 112 years before Constantine's conversion.

The full collections of the Beatty and the Bodmer papyri contain the majority of the New Testament, and *no* changes that can be construed as "Roman" are evident between these and post-Constantine copies. The conclusion: The Romans didn't entertain such motives and didn't take such actions.

74
Why does the epistle of Jude quote from the non-biblical book of Enoch?

Jude 14–15 (NKJV) says, "Now Enoch, the seventh from Adam, prophesied about these men also, saying, 'Behold, the Lord comes with ten thousands of His saints, to execute judgment on all, to convict all who are ungodly among them of all their ungodly deeds which they have committed in an ungodly way, and of all the harsh things which ungodly sinners have spoken against Him.'"

This prophecy isn't from the Old Testament but from the non-biblical Book 1 of Enoch, which—though purportedly written by the Enoch of Genesis 5:24—didn't exist until about two centuries before Christ. So why did Jude quote from it as if it were inspired by God? Well, just because he quoted a sentence from it doesn't mean he considered the *entire* book inspired. He was simply quoting a well-known statement that proved his point.

The apostle Paul often quoted Greek authors for the same reason. For example, Paul wrote, "One of them, a prophet of their own, said, 'Cretans are always liars, evil beasts, lazy gluttons.' This testimony is true" (Titus 1:12–13 NKJV). Paul was quoting *Cretica* by Epimenides (500s BC), a Cretan poet said to have made several true predictions. Does this mean Paul endorsed everything Epimenides said? By no means! In *Cretica*, Epimenides wrote of Zeus, "thou livest and abidest forever." Of course, Paul wouldn't have agreed with that statement—or used it in one of his letters.

Acts 17:28 also records Paul quoting Epimenides and also citing the Cilician poet Aratus (315–240 BC). In 1 Corinthians 15:33, he quoted the play *Thais* by the Greek playwright Menander (342–291 BC). *Thais* was a comedy about a prostitute—so Paul obviously would not have considered it God-inspired. It's unlikely he even watched the play. The quote he repeated was a common proverb among Greeks of his day.

75
Why were the Gnostic "gospels" excluded from the New Testament?

What most people know about Gnosticism is what they learn from reading the book *The Da Vinci Code* or from watching TV documentaries on the subject. The impression these works give is that Gnostics were simply spiritually minded Christians seeking to know God (the Greek word *gnōsis* means "knowledge"), enjoy religious freedom, and worship "the divine feminine." When you sit down to study their writings, however, you're in for some very bizarre reading.

Gnostics wrote the "gospels" of Thomas, Philip, Judas, Mary, etc., and some recent works insist that the early Church wrongfully excluded the "truths" of the Gnostic gospels from the New Testament. Such TV shows and books leave the impression that the Gnostic gospels show us what the "real" and "very human" Jesus was like.

The opposite is true, however. The historical Gospels—Matthew, Mark, Luke, and John—describe Jesus as real and very human. They speak of Him being hungry, thirsty, tired, and angry. The Gnostic gospels, on the other hand, describe Him as a disembodied spirit who only *appeared* to have a body. Instead of healing the sick and feeding the hungry, the Gnostic "Jesus" rambles on and on in long, esoteric philosophical discourses.

The Gospel of Thomas is merely a collection of sayings Jesus supposedly said, whereas the Secret Book According to John contains intellectual speculation on endless spiritual realms and ages and so-called manifestations of God. It distorts Jesus' simple Gospel into something unspeakably complex.

Gnostics were *not*, as some claim, the first Christians. They appeared some sixty years after Christ, and it wasn't before AD 130 that they had fully developed their theology. Gnostics wrote their spurious "gospels" in the second century AD, fraudulently claiming that Thomas, Mary Magdalene, and Judas had written them earlier.

The leaders of the early Church easily recognized these writings as non-historical frauds, and therefore excluded them from the New Testament canon.

One final question:
What will I do about Jesus?

If you're a Christian, I trust that these Q&As have strengthened your faith, "so you can be certain of the truth of everything you were taught" (Luke 1:4 NLT).

Yes, Christianity is solidly rooted in real time. It is a historical faith, one that has time and again been validated by archaeological discoveries. The writers of the New Testament were eyewitnesses of the events they describe. As the apostle Peter wrote, "We have not followed cunningly devised fables, when we made known unto you the power and coming of our Lord Jesus Christ, but were eyewitnesses" (2 Peter 1:16 KJV).

If you're not yet a Christian, then here's a question you might want to ponder: "What then shall I do with Jesus who is called Christ?" (Matthew 27:22 NKJV). As you have seen, there are answers to questions people have about the Bible. I hope that you've seen that trusting in Jesus Christ doesn't mean shutting off your mind and ignoring reason. It's not a leap in the dark. Christianity is understandable and makes sense. The apostle Paul declared that it is "true and reasonable" (Acts 26:25 NIV).

The four Gospels are historical accounts of the life of Jesus. They also testify that He has power to perform miracles. But more than anything, they were "written that you may believe that Jesus is the Christ, the Son of God, and that believing you may have life in His name" (John 20:31 NKJV). How do you do this? "If you confess with your mouth that Jesus is Lord and believe in your heart that God raised him from the dead, you will be saved. For it is by believing in your heart that you are made right with God, and it is by confessing with your mouth that you are saved" (Romans 10:9–10 NLT).

Understand Your Bible

John A. Beck

In loving memory of my mother,
Lorraine Beck,
who led me to love and to understand
God's Word.

Contents

Introduction

Does your desire to read the Bible often clash with the frustration you feel when you do? The Bible is the bestselling book of all time, which means it's likely there is at least one Bible in almost every home in America. But it's also very likely that those Bibles go unread, in part because the Bible can be difficult to understand. If this describes your situation and you have a desire to dig more deeply into God's Word, then you've come to the right place.

An unread Bible is like an unopened treasure chest because it contains precious insights that can be acquired from no other source. In the pages of scripture, God tenderly addresses our feelings of guilt and shame. He offers advice on improving our relationships and on raising our children. He reveals the pathway of wisdom and the secrets of true success. He offers vital words of encouragement when we're down and can't see a way out of our difficult circumstances. And He reveals His deep love for us and His desire to know us intimately—and for us to know Him. Given all that we have to gain, it makes sense that we would want to find the key to this bounty of spiritual treasure.

The Bible Can Be Clear

In many places, the language of the Bible is unmistakably plain, leaving no room for misinterpretation. For example, when the Bible describes the consequences of our sinful rebellion, it is both straightforward and startling: "The wages of sin is death" (Romans 6:23). Fortunately, the solution to this crisis is presented in language that is crystal clear and comforting: "For God so loved the world that he gave his one and only Son, that whoever believes in him shall not perish but have eternal life" (John 3:16). The same can be said for this divinely inspired declaration of support found in Psalm 46:1: "God is our refuge and strength, an ever-present help in trouble."

The Bible Can Be Confusing

For every clear passage we find in the Bible, it seems there are dozens that challenge and even confound our understanding. For example, what are we to make of this passage from the Law given in Deuteronomy? "Count off seven weeks from the time you begin to put the sickle to the standing grain. Then celebrate the Festival of Weeks to the LORD your God by giving a freewill offering in proportion to the blessing the LORD your God has given you" (Deuteronomy 16:9–10).

Or what can we glean from the long lists of people or places that fill entire pages of our Bibles? The second half of Joshua is notorious for such lists. "This is the inheritance of the tribe of Judah, according to its clans: The southernmost towns of the tribe of Judah in the Negev toward the boundary of Edom were: Kabzeel, Eder, Jagur, Kinah, Dimonah, Adadah, Kedesh, Hazor, Ithnan. . ." (Joshua 15:20–23).

Even words from the mouth of Jesus can be confusing: "Salt is good, but if it loses its saltiness, how can it be made salty again? It is fit neither for the soil nor for the manure pile;

it is thrown out" (Luke 14:34–35).

The Bible is supposed to help us; but passages like these can leave us confused and frustrated. For many people, this means the Bible goes back on the shelf, where it does no good at all.

The Bible Acknowledges It Can Be Confusing

It is striking, and somewhat comforting to know, that the Bible acknowledges how difficult it can be to understand. The author of Acts introduces us to a confused Bible reader, a well-educated man from the royal court of Ethiopia who had come to Jerusalem to worship in the days following the death and resurrection of Jesus. There is no doubt that, during his visit, he would have heard the news of a man named Jesus who identified Himself as the promised Savior of the world and who had miraculously risen from the dead three days after His crucifixion.

As the royal official's chariot bounced from rut to rut on the way home, the man was quietly reading his Bible, trying to make sense of it all. The Holy Spirit directed Philip, a close follower of Jesus, to walk down the same road and approach the chariot. The puzzled look on the Ethiopian's face betrayed the confusion raging in his mind. This prompted Philip to ask a probing question: "Do you understand what you are reading?" "How can I," the man replied, "unless someone explains it to me?" (Acts 8:30–31).

There you have it. The Bible acknowledges the problem. If a motivated, intelligent reader who lived during the first century—at the very time that some of the events of the Bible were unfolding—can meet obstacles in his Bible reading, we should not feel ashamed when we struggle to understand a portion of God's Word.

This Book Addresses
Bible-Reading Confusion

This book has the same goal that Philip had on that desert road: to address the confusion that can accompany Bible reading. At the risk of oversimplification, we can group common misunderstandings of the Bible into six categories, which we will then address in the following six chapters.

In chapter 1 we will answer the question, *What is the Bible?* Our focus will be on both the human and divine sides of its origins. We will consider how the unique beginnings of this book call for us to read the Bible in a way that we read no other book. At times our frustration in reading a Bible passage can be the result of our failure to consider the small details in the larger context of the big ideas that God wants to share with us.

The second chapter introduces five big ideas that God shares again and again in the Bible. We will see how reading passages that confuse us in light of these big ideas can improve our understanding and help us to answer the question, *What is God talking about?*

The third chapter raises the question, *How is God speaking?* Although the Bible is bound as a single volume and conveys the message of a single author—that is, God Himself—the style of writing varies from book to book and can even change within a book. Some of our confusion in reading the Bible can be attributed to reading one type of writing with rules meant to apply to another. Chapter 3 introduces the primary categories of literature (genres) we find in the Bible and offers general suggestions on how to read each most profitably.

The fourth chapter is governed by the question, *What is going on behind the scenes?* In almost all cases, the depth of our understanding will grow when we develop a better understanding of historical context. This is certainly true when we read the New Testament epistles—ancient letters delivered to specific people living in a specific place at a specific time and dealing with specific issues. But it is also true of Bible stories in general that a broader understanding of the historical context will shed light on the words and actions found in the narrative.

Cultural context can be as important to our understanding of the Bible as historical context. That's why in chapter 5 we'll tackle the question, *What are they doing?* Because the Bible describes the lives of people who lived in a distant land and far removed from our modern age, we can expect to find references to food, dress, manners, and customs that are very different from our own. The description of such practices and devices, as well as their use in figures of speech, may challenge our understanding until we deepen our awareness of the Bible's cultural context.

Finally, we'll come to the question, *Where am I?* Many Bible passages include place names and descriptions of topography, geology, water, flora, fauna, and the ways that people responded to the physical setting in which they lived. Chapter 6 illustrates the value of deepening our awareness of geographical context.

"Do You Understand
What You Are Reading?"

You may not be reading your Bible while bouncing along in a chariot after a visit to Jerusalem. But like the Ethiopian official, you may be challenged and frustrated by not being able to fully comprehend what God is saying in the Bible. My prayer is that the following discussion will give new direction to your Bible reading and will lead to rewarding insights and a greater passion to read your Bible on a regular basis. Read on—exciting discoveries lie just ahead!

What Is the Bible?

When we meet someone for the first time, our early exchanges are often governed by carefully choreographed questions through which we learn more about one another. *Where do you live? Where did you go to school? What do you do for a living?* The answers to these and other questions about family, interests, and hobbies provide the foundation for friendship and further interaction.

The information we gather when meeting someone new is similar to the information gathering we do when we pick up a book for the first time. We turn it over in our hands and examine the cover, the table of contents, and the author's biography to get some idea of what the book is all about and whether a sustained "conversation" with the author might be worth our time.

Our approach to the Bible is no different. To understand what the Bible says, we would do well first to ask, "What is it?" The Bible looks very much like any other book—whether it's one we've pulled from the shelf, downloaded onto a portable reading device, or opened on a computer screen. Yet the truth of the matter is that the Bible is different from the children's books in our kids' rooms; different from our college textbooks, our technical manuals, and our novels; and different from the cookbooks in the kitchen.

In this chapter we will see that the Bible is a very unique book, because it has both a divine and a human side to its origins. We'll take a look at the Bible's unique origins, see the important implications of those origins, and illustrate how knowing what the Bible *is* will change the way we read and engage with its contents.

The Human Side

Experience teaches that a well-crafted page of writing, with appropriately formed sentences and paragraphs, is not produced by plants or random animals. Neither is it the product of a strong wind blowing arbitrary words off the page of a dictionary. So when we look at the pages of the Bible, we can safely assume that a human author has been at work. The truth of the matter is that the Bible has many human authors, representing a wide range of times, places, occupations, and circumstances.

Moses is widely regarded as the author of the first five books of the Bible. He started writing in about 1450 BC. On a timeline, that's more than 2,800 years before the invention of the printing press, nearly 3,200 years before the signing of the U.S. Constitution, and more than 3,400 years before today. At the other end of the spectrum, the most recent books of the Bible date to the first century AD—closer to our modern day, but still nearly 2,000 years removed. To sum it all up, the sixty-six books of the Bible were composed by a variety of human authors between the fifteenth century BC and the first century AD—a span of more than 1,500 years.

When they wrote they put pen to paper in many different locations, from Africa to the Middle East, and from Europe to Asia. As we might expect, some of the books were written within the borders of the Promised Land, Israel. Other writers of the Bible wrote in places as distant and distinct as Egypt, Babylon (modern-day Iraq), Asia Minor (modern-day Turkey), and Corinth (which is in Greece).

The writers of the Bible also came from a variety of backgrounds. Some were leaders, such as Moses and Samuel; or prophets, such as Isaiah, Jeremiah, Ezekiel, and Obadiah. But also among the recognized writers we find kings, such as David and Solomon; a physician (Luke); a Roman tax collector (Matthew); fishermen, such as Peter and John; and Amos, who identifies himself as both a shepherd and a fig farmer (see Amos 7:14).

Coming, as they did, from across the timeline and geographical boundaries of the ancient world, the authors of the books of the Bible composed their poetry and prose from a wide range of personal circumstances. They knew both good times and bad. Some had celebrated the birth of children; others had experienced the heady rewards of business or political success. We also meet authors whose lives were beset by personal tragedy—the loss of a child, a wayward wife, or exile in a foreign country. We meet some who are struggling spiritually in the wake of serious sins like murder or adultery. Still others had to deal with rebellious children, personal depression, military invasion, or time spent in prison. As real people living in real places in real time, the authors of the Bible saw life in all its glory and all its disappointments.

The Implications
of Human Authorship

Because the human authors of the Bible experienced life in all its fullness, we feel the humanness in what they've written. We resonate with their joys and feel the wrenching of their sorrows. We hear their laughter and see the tears that stained the pages on which they wrote. We rejoice in their victories and feel the disappointment of the losses that threatened to rob them of hope. In all these experiences and feelings—which are very real to us—we can quickly and easily immerse ourselves in the pages of this great book.

The Divine Side

What makes the Bible so unique is that it also has a divine side to its origins. The eternal God, who is both creator and ultimate ruler of our world, clearly has a passion to speak to us. Though He has spoken individually and directly to people in the past—or at least as directly as we mortals can endure—in most cases, God has chosen to communicate in writing, using a very unique process of composition that involves both a human and a divine author working in concert.

Within the Bible we find reference to this unique phenomenon, which has been called *divine inspiration*. Just as God animated the lifeless flesh of the first human being by breathing into his nostrils "the breath of life" (Genesis 2:7), so we are told that "all Scripture is God-breathed" (2 Timothy 3:16). The human authors of the Bible who received this "breath of God" tapped in to a knowledge base bigger than their own. The apostle Paul puts it this way in 1 Corinthians 2:13: "This is what we speak, not in words taught us by human wisdom but in words taught by the Spirit, explaining spiritual realities with Spirit-taught words." At times we get the impression that these human authors were barely keeping up during this process. Peter says, "Prophets, though human, spoke from God as they were carried along by the Holy Spirit" (2 Peter 1:21).

The phrase *divine inspiration* captures the essence and mystery of the process. The English word *inspiration* comes from the Latin *inspirare*, which means "to breathe in." In this case inspiration is not merely a brilliant flash of insight. It is more than the ability to scan the horizon of the human experience and capture the essentials with just the right words. The writing process that resulted in the Bible was both informed and directed by the Holy Spirit. In the end God communicated precisely what He intended to say, yet in ways that reflected the unique experiences, knowledge, perceptions, and writing styles of the human authors. God spoke through these writers, yet without abolishing the uniqueness of their human contribution.

The Implications of Divine Authorship

If you're a bit confused by this description of the biblical writing process, that's not surprising. No one fully understands how God accomplished His purpose in giving us the Bible, but we can quickly see the implications and the importance of divine authorship. First of all, it means that what we read in the Bible is true. Left to their own devices, the human authors of the Bible were entirely capable of selecting the wrong word or of making a mistake in reporting the details of an event. God, on the other hand, is incapable of error. As the Holy Spirit directed the writing process, He made sure that these authors rose above the horizon of their mortal limitations so that what they wrote came to us in untarnished form.

When Jesus prayed for His disciples, He called attention to this striking quality of divine speech: "Sanctify them by the truth; your word is truth" (John 17:17). Though the Bible was written thousands of years ago, in a time before computers, cameras, and video recorders, we can be assured that these writers knew what they were talking about because their writing was overseen by God Himself. God's Word is true.

The Bible's truthfulness and reliability make it a "must read" book. Other books may rise quickly on the *New York Times* bestseller list and clamor for our attention. Such well-crafted books have the power to entertain, inform, and guide us. But every one of those books fails to rise above human limitations. Only in the Bible do we hear God speaking to us directly and candidly. Of all the books that have ever been published—or that ever will be published—the Bible is the only one we *must* read and understand.

Illustration

Because the Bible has such a unique heritage, we read it differently than we do other books. When we read an ordinary book, we evaluate its integrity based on our knowledge of the author and his or her credentials—particularly when the author is challenging us to think or act in a certain way. For example, if I'm reading a book about raising my kids, I'm going to reserve judgment on the book's usefulness and value until I've evaluated the author's knowledge, expertise, and approach. If the author makes suggestions that fall outside the realm of what seems practical or credible, that book is likely to find itself on the resale shelf. The unique origins of the Bible, on the other hand, change the way we read and respond to its message and application. Because of its divine authorship, presented through the lives and words of human writers, the Bible can challenge us to believe the unbelievable and do the unthinkable.

Heavenly Math

God makes every effort to reveal His true identity within the pages of the Bible. Yet we can have difficulty understanding what He is telling us. In some places the Bible clearly declares that God is one: "Hear, O Israel: The LORD our God, the LORD is one" (Deuteronomy 6:4). In other places God speaks of Himself in the plural (see Genesis 1:26), and Jesus calls for the recognition of God as three distinct persons: "Therefore go and make disciples of all nations, baptizing them in the name of the Father and of the Son and of the Holy Spirit" (Matthew 28:19).

So is God three or is God one? Our earthbound math limits us to one of those two options. But the God who created our world—and mathematics—lives beyond such limitations. That's why He can describe Himself as both three and one at the same time: $1 + 1 + 1 = 1$. If I were reading any other book, I might quickly dismiss that idea as preposterous. Yet, because I know that "the foolishness of God is wiser than human wisdom" (1 Corinthians 1:25), I read the Bible in a different way. When I recognize the Bible as God's own book, I can ponder these equations and nod my head in agreement, marveling at a mystery that exceeds my comprehension.

Radical Love

The Bible not only calls for us to believe the unbelievable, but it also can call us to do the unthinkable. Each day, we make decisions—both consciously and unconsciously—about how we will treat the people around us. As we interact with other drivers on the roadway, with sales clerks at the store, and with our family members, we naturally fall into patterns of extending varying degrees of kindness and courtesy to those who cross our path. If we are honest with ourselves, we tend to reserve the best treatment for those who have proven themselves worthy. In the Bible Jesus calls for us to rethink our habits of interaction. "You have heard that it was said, 'Love your neighbor and hate your enemy.' But I tell you, love your enemies and pray for those who persecute you, that you may be children of your Father in heaven. He causes his sun to rise on the evil and the good, and sends rain on the righteous and the unrighteous" (Matthew 5:43–45). Common sense might suggest that this is an unthinkable course of action. Should we not reward those who treat us well with the best treatment and withhold kindness from those who mean us harm? But here the Bible encourages us to take God's perspective—to lavish sunshine and rain on those who treat Him well and those who do not. As the Bible calls for us to believe the unbelievable, it also calls for us to do what at first blush seems unthinkable.

Bible References

As a book the Bible is somewhat unique in that it has a tiered set of divisions, which allows quick reference to even its shortest parts.

First, the Bible is divided into two testaments. Generally speaking, the Old Testament is the collection of writings that introduce us to God and to His plan to rescue the world from sin. The New Testament speaks about the realization of the promises made in the Old Testament, focusing largely on the life of Jesus and the history of the Church that took shape around His teachings.

Each of the two testaments is divided into books—thirty-nine in the Old Testament and twenty-seven in the New Testament, for a total of sixty-six. When a Bible reference is given, the first element in the reference is to one of these books.

Each book in the Bible is further divided into chapters, and each chapter is subdivided into verses. If someone wishes to call attention to a specific sentence or paragraph in the Bible, he or she will typically not use a page number (which varies from one version of the Bible to the next), but will point to the reference by identifying the book, chapter, and verse(s). It will look like this: Matthew 5:1–12. In this case, the reference is to the New Testament book of Matthew, chapter 5, verses 1 through 12.

English Versions

The human authors of the Bible expressed themselves in three languages—Hebrew, Aramaic, and Greek—all of which are unfamiliar to most modern readers. That means our English versions are translations from those languages.

If you read the same Bible passage in more than one English version, you will likely find some differences. English translations differ from one another in two ways. First, the Bible translators worked with principles that guided their translation efforts for a particular version. Sometimes the goal is to remain as close as possible to the language structure of the parent text, even if that makes the translation sound somewhat less natural to native English speakers. Alternatively, the translator may have sought to produce a translation that sounds very natural in English, even if it diverges from the original images and language structure of the parent text.

Bible translations also vary from one another in that they are targeting the vocabulary and style of a particular group of English speakers. Vocabulary and grammar change with time and location and within subgroups that live within a certain time and place. For that reason the translators must choose a particular form of English to use, to make their translation readable by their intended audience. So, for example, the King James Version of the Bible was written in the style of

English used in Great Britain in the seventeenth century, and the New Living Translation is written in more contemporary, modern English.

Each type of translation has its place. If you would like to learn more about the translation philosophy that guided your English translation, read the preface of your Bible. This is where the Bible's publisher typically discusses the translation philosophy that guided their version of the Bible.

Bible reading can become very frustrating when we get bogged down in sentences, paragraphs, or even pages filled with apparently meaningless details. When we encounter portions of God's Word like this, we may well ask, "What is God talking about?" In many respects, it is like joining a conversation that is already in progress. At first all we may hear in the conversation are references to people, places, and actions that seem unrelated to one another. Only after we have listened for a while and understand the bigger ideas being discussed can we make sense of the smaller details. The same is true of our Bible reading. It is most helpful to know the big ideas that God shares with us in the Bible so that the smaller details can find their place among them.

The Obstacle

Some sections of the Bible come at us like an avalanche. The images and ideas tumble over one another and threaten to sweep us off the mountain, turning us head over heels before burying us in the suffocating darkness of too much detail. That verbal avalanche often strikes us when we read a chapter that contains a long list of laws, some of which sound particularly strange to the modern ear:

"Do not cook a young goat in its mother's milk" (Exodus 34:26).

"Keep my decrees. Do not mate different kinds of animals" (Leviticus 19:19).

"Do not eat any meat with the blood still in it" (Leviticus 19:26).

"Do not plow with an ox and a donkey yoked together. Do not wear clothes of wool and linen woven together" (Deuteronomy 22:10–11).

In other sections of the Bible, we encounter long lists of unfamiliar place names to which we have no apparent connection. For example, "The allotment for the trip of Judah, according to its clans, extended down to the territory of Edom, to the Desert of Zin in the extreme south. Their southern boundary started from the bay the at the southern end of the Dead Sea, crossed south of Scorpion Pass, continued on to Zin and went over to the south of Kadesh Barnea" (Joshua 15:1–3).

In still other passages, we encounter lists of people's names, such as in the first chapter of Matthew: "This is the genealogy of Jesus the Messiah the son of David, the son of Abraham: Abraham was the father of Isaac, Isaac the father of Jacob, Jacob the father of Judah and his brothers, Judah the father of Perez and Zerah, whose mother was Tamar, Perez the father of Hezron, Hezron the father of Ram. . ." (Matthew 1:1–3). We rightly presume that God has something to say to us here, but what is it?

The Solution

We can understand the role of Bible passages like these when we become familiar with the five big ideas that God shares with us in His Word. Though the Bible generally moves forward in time from the book of Genesis through the book of Revelation, it also circles back to repeat and emphasize the big ideas that God longs to share with us in our conversation with Him. We will better understand everything in the Bible when we read it with an awareness of those big ideas. Let's consider each in turn.

1. There Is Only One God.

The authors of the Bible, whether they lived during the time of the Old Testament or the New Testament, lived amid cultures that believed in many gods—multiple deities who competed with one another, often at the expense of us mere mortals.

In complete contrast the Bible affirms that there is just one God. In the very first verse of the Bible, Genesis 1:1, this one God is identified as the creator of all things. There is absolutely no mention of other deities on the eternal stage, either competing with God or supporting His efforts. In the Law of Moses, the very first commandment turns this idea into a divine directive: "You shall have no other gods before me. You shall not make for yourself an image in the form of anything in heaven above or on the earth beneath or in the waters below. You shall not bow down to them or worship them" (Exodus 20:3–5).

This big idea, which is introduced so aggressively in the first two books of the Bible, is repeated again and again in the books that follow. At times this idea is presented directly:

"Hear, O Israel: The LORD our God, the LORD is one" (Deuteronomy 6:4).

"This is what the LORD says—Israel's King and Redeemer, the LORD Almighty: I am the first and I am the last; apart from me there is no God" (Isaiah 44:6).

At other times it is presented as a warning to avoid building and worshipping images that represent the fraudulent deities of the surrounding culture:

"All who make idols are nothing, and the things they treasure are worthless. Those who would speak up for them are blind; they are ignorant, to their own shame" (Isaiah 44:9).

"Do I mean then that food sacrificed to an idol is anything, or that an idol is anything? No, but the sacrifices of pagans are offered to demons, not to God, and I do not want you to be participants with demons" (1 Corinthians 10:19–20).

The first big idea is clear: There is only one God.

2. God Is Holy, and He Demands That We Be Holy.

To be holy is to be unique or set apart from the ordinary. This is a fundamental quality of God's, which He imparted to mortals on the day of their creation (Genesis 1:27). This does not mean that Adam and Eve were gods, but it does mean they were created so that their native passions, desires, and actions were in harmony with God's. So long as Adam and Eve remained holy, as God is holy, they could enjoy His company. However, when they experimented with thinking and actions contrary to God's will, they plunged themselves and their descendants into an unholy state, at enmity with God. As this ruined condition spread down through the generations, it had its impact on the environment and on the human condition. Physical pain, strained relationships, weeds in the garden, and the death of those we love are reminders that things changed for the worse after the Fall (see Genesis 3:14–19).

Even though this change in state occurred for humanity, the prime directive from God had not changed: "Be holy because I, the LORD your God, am holy" (Leviticus 19:2). God is not suggesting that we just do the best we can under the circumstances. No, His standard is still perfection. The legal directives that fill the Bible are a reminder of all that God requires. But we all find ourselves in the same situation that the apostle Paul found himself: "For I do not do the good I want to do, but the evil I do not want to do—this I keep on doing" (Romans 7:19). This second big idea—that God is holy and demands that every mortal be holy as well—creates a real dilemma for us.

3. God Has a Plan to Restore Us to Holiness.

This idea is perhaps the biggest of the big ideas presented in the Bible, because it so radically changes the future of all who will accept it. God's solution to our sin resides in the core principle of *substitution*. As a just God who put the earlier foundation principle in place, God was obligated to punish the rebellion that mortal humans introduced into the world. But He also had a solution to the problem: He could provide a substitute to stand in the place of those who owed God a perfect life but could no longer deliver on their obligation. Furthermore, this substitute, though undeserving of any punishment Himself, would be punished on our behalf, so that the divine obligation to punish sin would no longer be hanging over our heads. In the Old Testament, Isaiah anticipates the coming of this substitute, Jesus, with vivid language: "Surely he took up our pain and bore our suffering, yet we considered him punished by God, stricken by him, and afflicted. But he was pierced for our transgressions, he was crushed for our iniquities; the punishment that brought us peace was on him, and by his wounds we are healed. We all, like sheep, have gone astray, each of us has turned to our own way; and the LORD has laid on him the iniquity of us all" (Isaiah 53:4–6).

In 2 Corinthians 5:21 the apostle Paul looks back on the life of Jesus and expresses the big idea of substitution in this way: "God made him who had no sin to be sin for us, so that in him we might become the righteousness of God." And what does God ask in payment to receive the benefits of this plan? He asks only that we believe what He has said about us. We are again holy in God's eyes because Jesus did what we could not do and undid what we had done.

God's plan to provide a substitute is mentioned immediately after Adam and Eve exchanged their holy state for a sinful state (see Genesis 3:15). As we turn through the pages of the Old Testament, we see the promised plan for substitution described with increasing detail. For example, the Lord appears to Abram and tells him that, although he is childless at the moment, his offspring will grow to become a great nation. God further promises Abram that his family-turned-nation will occupy a special piece of real estate, the Promised Land of Canaan. Finally, Abram is told that the Savior from sin, the substitute for all mortals, will be a descendant of that nation and be born in the Promised Land (see Genesis 12:1–3). Throughout the Old Testament, the ideas of "nation" and "land" are intimately linked to the big idea of salvation by substitution.

The promise is further narrowed and focused after the nation of Israel has been formed and King David is ruling as its king. He is told that the coming Savior (Messiah) will be one of his descendants. So, from this time on, the biblical authors also use royal imagery when speaking about the coming of this special substitute. He would be the King who rules an eternal kingdom (see 2 Samuel 7:11–16). The world was holding its breath, waiting for the arrival of this special substitute, when the angel Gabriel appeared to a young girl in the small agricultural village of Nazareth. He had special news for Mary: "You will conceive and give birth to a son, and you are to call him Jesus. He will be great and will be called the Son of the Most High. The Lord God will give him the throne of his father David, and he will reign over Jacob's descendants forever; his kingdom will never end" (Luke 1:31–33).

Jesus did exactly what we needed Him to do for us. He intervened to live the life we owed God but could not deliver; He is the one who absorbed the punishment of God headed our way. Paul sums up this big idea in one powerful sentence: "For just as through the disobedience of the one man the many were made sinners, so also through the obedience of the one man the many will be made righteous" (Romans 5:19). This remains the biggest of the big ideas in the Bible.

4. God Wants Us to Enjoy Successful Lives on Earth.

Life goes on, and it can be full of challenges—in no small part because those who oppose the coming of God and His kingdom will do all they can to make life more difficult for God's people. How can we find greater success and happiness in the daily lives we lead? The human author of Ecclesiastes tried to find satisfaction and success on earth without turning to the direction that God offered. The result of that experiment in living is captured with words like these:

"I have seen all the things that are done under the sun; all of them are meaningless, a chasing after the wind" (Ecclesiastes 1:14).

"I denied myself nothing my eyes desired; I refused my heart no pleasure. My heart took delight in all my labor, and this was the reward for all my toil. Yet when I surveyed all that my hands had done and what I had toiled to achieve, everything was meaningless, a chasing after the wind; nothing was gained under the sun" (Ecclesiastes 2:10–11).

Life in a sin-ruined world can feel like chasing after the wind, even for those who know Jesus as their Savior. But God has no desire for us to live in that frustration. He wants us to find some measure of happiness and success, and so He offers direction for living in the world He created. Some of that direction comes to us in the form of commandments, such as the one that safeguards our personal property: "You shall not steal" (Exodus 20:15). At other times the lesson for living comes to us in story form. A vignette from the story of Joseph illustrates how one can successfully manage sexual temptation (see Genesis 39). The Proverbs are short axioms that offer general direction on successful living:

"The soothing tongue is a tree of life, but a perverse tongue crushes the spirit" (Proverbs 15:4).

"A hot-tempered person stirs up conflict, but the one who is patient calms the quarrel" (Proverbs 15:18).

Jesus encouraged a perspective change on life, which was designed to mitigate worry (see Matthew 6:25–34). God longs to show us how we can find greater success and happiness in a world that offers precious little of both—which leads us to the fifth and final big idea.

5. *God Has a Plan for Our Eternal Happiness.*

In the end the fullest realization of the happiness we seek will always run up against the cold reality that we are looking for perfection in an imperfect world. The fifth big idea presented in the Bible addresses the life that will follow the one we know on earth. Jesus demonstrated His power over death by rising from the tomb on the third day. Part of His plan for our eternal happiness involves the resurrection of our bodies, as well. In speaking with a grieving sister, Jesus laid that reality bare: "I am the resurrection and the life. The one who believes in me will live, even though they die; and who-ever lives by believing in me will never die" (John 11:25–26).

The new bodies we will enjoy after death will have a new home that is completely redeemed from the ruin of sin. The apostle John received a brief glimpse into this world. He found language inadequate to express all that he saw, but he shared what he could. In a revelation from God, John saw thousands of people in white robes and inquired about who they were. Here is the answer he received:

"These are they who have come out of the great tribulation; they have washed their robes and made them white in the blood of the Lamb. Therefore, they are before the throne of God and serve him day and night in his temple, and he who sits on the throne will shelter them with his presence. 'Never again will they hunger; never again will they thirst. The sun will not beat down on them,' nor any scorching heat. For the Lamb at the center of the throne will be their shepherd;

'he will lead them to springs of living water.' 'And God will wipe away every tear from their eyes' " (Revelation 7:14–17).

The final book of the Bible returns us to the same themes we found in the first chapter of the Bible. Humans will once again live in perfect harmony with their creator. God has a plan for our eternal happiness.

Illustration

When we encounter a set of verses that don't make much sense on their own, it can be most helpful to see their relationship to one or more of the five big ideas that God repeatedly communicates in His Word. Take, for example, the laws we mentioned earlier. Most of the laws found in the Old Testament were in effect only between the time when God issued them on Mount Sinai and when the Savior completed His work on earth. As promised, the family of Abraham grew to become a great nation. Each member of that nation became a caretaker of the most precious promise God had given the world, the promise to send a Savior. To remind Israel of their special assignment and to distinguish them from all the other nations of the world, God imposed a unique lifestyle on them. He called for them to be holy—that is, to live lives distinguishable from all the other nations of the world. They were to avoid eating meat with the blood still in it, refrain from plowing with an ox and a donkey yoked together, and not wear garments that combined wool and linen. These unique requirements reminded the nation that they were a unique people who served a unique God. These temporary laws that fill the early books of the Bible help us understand how God identified and maintained Israel as a unique people, a nest in which the promise of salvation was incubated.

The long lists of place names we find in the book of Joshua have a similar role to play. At the time of Abraham, the Lord tied the promise of the Savior to the Promised Land. As the one true God who created the world, the Lord had the right to assign property as He saw fit. It was the Lord's desire to make the promise of the coming Savior personal by giving each family a small segment of the Promised Land on which to build their home, grow their grain, and graze their animals. Property does not function for us in that way today; but in the Bible, owning a piece of the Promised Land was how a family could connect itself to God's plan to save the world.

Likewise, the long list of names that opens the book of Matthew plays a very important role in God's plan, as Matthew seeks to link the promises made in the Old Testament with their fulfillment in Jesus Christ. Given all that God had said about the coming Messiah, it became clear that the Savior could not be born into just any family. People such as Abraham, Jacob, Judah, and David had been promised that this special substitute would be a member of their family. In that light Matthew's list makes much more sense. The genealogy begins with Abraham and mentions all the key figures to whom the promise had been made. Joseph, Jesus' earthly father, is mentioned just before Jesus because, among the ancient Israelites, one's genealogical heritage was always traced through the father. So this list, which at first blush fails to engage us as readers, actually becomes an important key in identifying Jesus as the substitute sent by God to provide a pathway that restores our relationship with God.

Bible reading can become frustrating when we get bogged down by paragraphs filled with apparently meaningless details. But we can gain a better understanding of these challenging passages when we view them in light of the five big ideas that God desires to communicate in His conversation with us.

Our eyes touch a wide variety of reading materials in any given week, including business e-mails, advertisements, Tweets, software agreements, novels, and notes sent home from school. Nimbly and without giving it a thought, we change our reading speed, level of attention, and general engagement in order to properly adjust to the text before us. We need to make similar adjustments when we read the Bible. Although one page of the Bible can look very similar to the next, those pages often contain different categories of written communication or genre, which call for us to adjust the way we read them. To best understand what God says to us in His Word, we need to ask how He is speaking to us on a particular page and adjust our reading strategy to match.

The Obstacle

Because we are less familiar with the genres used by the biblical authors and less practiced at the art of reading them, we are less likely to make the necessary shifts in our reading and interpretation style as we move through the Bible. *Genre* is simply a fancy word for a category of writing using a similar style and form. We can think of genre as an unwritten agreement between the author and the reader. Each genre has its own set of reading rules that govern the relationship between reader and text. So, for example, we would read and understand a children's fairy tale in a different way than an online news magazine. If we fail to observe the rules of genre, we may leave the book of fairy tales believing that pigs can talk, that wolves dress in Grandma's clothing, and that one needs to be careful about climbing beanstalks grown from magic beans. Of course this sounds ridiculous, but we can make similar errors in our Bible reading when we try to read every page and every book in exactly the same way.

In the Bible, which encompasses several diverse genres, the shifts between genres can occur quickly and with little or no warning. Consider, for example, Judges 4–5. In these two chapters, the Bible describes the same event, the oppression of the Israelites by a Canaanite king and the divinely sponsored victory that released the Israelites from that oppression. In Judges 4 the author uses the genre of historical narrative to report on the event. In Judges 5 the same event is recast as an extended piece of poetry, which is a different genre with different rules. The use of two distinct literary forms to describe the same event serves to emphasize two different dimensions of the story. If we try to read both chapters with the same reading strategy, we are likely to miss what God is trying to tell us. That is why we need to ask, "How is God speaking?"

The Solution

We will read the Bible with greater understanding and greater satisfaction when we become familiar with the basic categories of literature, or genres, used, become familiar with the way the books are composed, and acquire basic strategies for reading and interpreting God's message to us. Here we will briefly introduce and illustrate the six types of communication we encounter most frequently in the Bible: historical narrative, poetry, law, prophecy, letters (epistles), and apocalyptic.

Historical Narrative

Historical narrative is the most commonly used genre in the Bible and is found in much of the Old Testament, in the Gospels, and in Acts. In this style of communication, the author takes historical events and turns them into a story. Because events are always composed of many more details than will fit in the story, the narrative approach involves a considerable amount of editing. Details of the event are reduced and organized by the author so that the story can be read in a reasonable amount of time and have the intended impact on its readers. This is not to say that the biblical authors distort the details of the event; however, they do condition our experience of the event in a number of ways, including organization of the details into a plot, strategic presentation of characters, and comments made by the narrator.

The inspired authors of the Bible organize their narratives into plots; by examining these plots, we can come to a better understanding of how the author intends for us to respond to the events in the story. The plot in most Bible stories consists of several standard components: crisis, complication, climax, and resolution. The crisis typically centers on a problem that inhibits the advance of God's kingdom or a problem faced by people living in every age. Once the crisis has been introduced, the author may report on circumstances that complicate the crisis and lead to a climax. At this point, God speaks or acts, either directly or via one of His earthly representatives, to resolve the matter. This carefully organized plot pattern helps maintain the reader's attention and directs it to the enduring lesson, a lesson that will be linked to the crisis resolution in the story.

Bible stories can cover many pages, but we will consider a brief story from Matthew 8 to illustrate the way in which a plot looks.

Then he [Jesus] got into the boat and his disciples followed him. Suddenly a furious storm came up on the lake, so that the waves swept over the boat. But Jesus was sleeping. The disciples went and woke him, saying, "Lord, save us! We're going to drown!"

He replied, "You of little faith, why are you so afraid?" Then he got up and rebuked the winds and the waves, and it was completely calm.

The men were amazed and asked, "What kind of man is this? Even the winds and the waves obey him!" (Matthew 8:23–27).

In a short story like this, the crisis is introduced quickly. An unexpected and violent windstorm unleashes its force against a boat full of men. The crisis is further complicated by the fact that Jesus is sleeping and by the words of the disciples, who give voice to their fear of drowning. The climax is reached when Jesus rises, rebukes the weather, and removes the threat. The disciples' rhetorical question—"What kind of man is this?"—directs us to the point of the narrative: As the Son of God, Jesus is capable of addressing threats to His people with a power that is truly out of this world.

Poetry

The poetry we read in the Bible flows from real-life events, but the authors of poetic passages typically spend more time directing our attention to the ideas behind the event than on the details of the event itself. The poet presents these ideas using an extreme economy of words, which changes the appearance of the communication on the page. Rather than long paragraphs, we find short lines filled with complex grammatical patterns, embellished with colorful imagery, filled with emotion, and embroidered with a variety of literary devices. In Psalm 1, for example, the inspired poet reflects on the great fortune enjoyed by one in the Lord's care. But rather than simply tell a narrative story, the poet turns the idea into images.

> *That person is like a tree*
> *planted by streams of water,*
> *which yields its fruit in season*
> *and whose leaf does not wither—*
> *whatever they do prospers.*
> PSALM 1:3

The nature of poetry changes the way we read it. While historical narrative encourages us to press on quickly from crisis to resolution so that we can discover the point or outcome of the story, poetry artfully presents an idea early in the poem and calls for us to stop and reflect almost as soon as we have begun. This type of reading calls for us to slow down, turn off life's distractions, and focus our thinking on the idea the poet wishes to share.

It will help our reading of biblical poetry to understand how the ancient Hebrews composed their poetry. Rather than using rhyme as a primary tool, they were more apt to employ repetition, contrast, and parallel structure to develop their ideas, using combinations of two or three short lines. At times the poet uses the second line of poetry to repeat and therefore emphasize the idea of the first line. Consider this poetic call to action from the Psalms:

> *Who will rise up for me against the wicked?*
> *Who will take a stand for me*
> *against evildoers?*
> PSALM 94:16

The biblical poets may also urge our consideration of an idea by using the second line in contrast to the first. In Psalm 1 the primary idea of God's care is contrasted with the experience of the wicked.

> *For the LORD watches over the way of the righteous,*
> *but the way of the wicked leads to destruction.*
> PSALM 1:6

A third way the initial idea can be developed is by introducing the idea in the first line and then expanding it in the following lines of poetry.

> *Blessed is the one*
> *who does not walk in step*
> *with the wicked*

or stand in the way that sinners take
or sit in the company of mockers.
PSALM 1:1

Recognizing that bad company can corrupt a good person, the inspired poet invites God's people to consider the company they keep and the level of contact they maintain with those who oppose the Lord. The three verbs used in these three poetic lines describe a progressive association, from "walking" to "standing" to "sitting." The blessed person avoids not only the most sustained contact with bad company—sitting—but even the most casual: walking.

These are just a few of the many patterns and literary devices in the poet's toolbox. Practice and sustained reading of biblical poetry will help us discover even more of these literary conventions. The key is to read slowly, reread, and observe the artful ways in which the poet presents, emphasizes, and develops an idea for our reflection.

Law

In stark contrast to poetry, laws in the Bible are presented in straightforward language without literary adornment. The laws in the Bible directly call the people of God to holiness. They directly summon us to consider our relationship to God, to other people, and to the natural environment in which we live.

In some ways reading law is easier than reading historical narrative or poetry; but one challenge that modern Bible readers face is how to determine whether the directives we find in the Law are time limited or universally applicable. Many of the laws found in the Old Testament represent God's will for a specific period of history. For example, in an earlier era, God clearly regulated the diet of the Israelites by prohibiting the consumption of pork (see Leviticus 11:7). In the New Testament era, following the death of Jesus, this command was no longer in force (see Acts 10:9–23). One can now be holy and still have pork for dinner. By contrast, certain laws pertain to everyone down through the ages. For example, God prohibits stealing, whether we live in the twenty-first century AD or the fourteenth century BC (see Deuteronomy 5:19).

Other cases are a bit more complex because we find a law meant to apply to all time presented in language of an earlier era. Consider the following directive, which calls for a weekly day of rest: "Observe the Sabbath day by keeping it holy, as the LORD your God has commanded you. Six days you shall labor and do all your work, but the seventh day is a sabbath to the LORD your God. On it you shall not do any work, neither you, nor your son or daughter, nor your male or female servant, nor your ox, your donkey or any of your animals, nor any foreigner residing in your towns, so that your male and female servants may rest, as you do" (Deuteronomy 5:12–14). Though we may not have servants or donkeys to help us maintain our homes, and we may not raise our own food, we can find a principle in this directive that applies universally to all time. God calls for us to set aside one day a week and free it from the mundane tasks that normally fill our days. The Jewish Sabbath was on Saturday, a day that most Christians no longer observe as Sabbath. Nevertheless, the principle of resting one day a week endures. To understand this genre of biblical communication, we again need to look for the controlling idea in the Law and determine if and how it applies to us in our era.

Prophecy

The prophets were God's selected representatives who were directed to speak to Old Testament Israel on God's behalf. In some cases the Lord intended for these individuals to write down their message and preserve it for future generations to read. These became the prophetic books that are named after the individual prophets—Isaiah, Jeremiah, Jonah, Haggai, and so on. We might expect such books to be filled with predictions about the future—and in some cases we do find language that speaks of a coming Messiah and a new, trouble-free age. But in most cases the prophetic writers were charged with responding to their immediate circumstances, often criticizing the attitudes and behaviors of their audience and illustrating the relationship between their habits and their distressed circumstances. When God's people repented, the prophets were quick to offer their listeners the hope that flows from a forgiving God.

Several strategies will allow us to read the prophetic books in a more informed way. First of all, most were written in poetic form. This means that the rules for reading and interpreting poetry apply here. By using poetry, the prophets show that their emphasis is often more on an idea than an event. Our goal as readers is to find the controlling idea, examine the artful way in which the poet repeats and develops it, and reflect on its application in our lives. Because the prophets most often write in response to certain historical events, it is also helpful for us to become aware of the historical circumstances behind their writing, so that we can set their ideas in the context of the events that surround them. Early in most of the prophetic books, we find some clues as to the particular era in which the message was given, if not the specific circumstances that motivated it. We can then turn to the companion portions of historical narrative, where we might learn more about the context that gave birth to the prophetic lesson we are reading. Finally, it is helpful to read larger segments of the prophetic books in one sitting, if not the entire book itself. Because the prophetic authors frequently repeat the controlling ideas, we may find that segments of the book that seem less clear may become clearer within the context of the whole.

Take the prophet Amos as an example. The first verses of his book help to situate the prophet in a very specific time frame (see Amos 1:1). Reading the companion historical narrative from 2 Kings and 2 Chronicles suggests that this was a more prosperous time economically for God's people, but also a time of greater idolatry and a time when the advantaged members of society were taking advantage of the disadvantaged. Amos lays bare the problem and the consequences to come:

> *This is what the LORD says:*
> *"For three sins of Israel,*
> *even for four, I will not relent.*
> *They sell the innocent for silver,*

> *and the needy for a pair of sandals.*
> *They trample on the heads of the poor*
> *as on the dust of the ground*
> *and deny justice to the oppressed. . . .*
> *"Now then, I will crush you*
> *as a cart crushes when loaded*
> *with grain."*
> AMOS 2:6–7, 13

With words like these, Amos highlighted the social injustice rampant in the land, built the case against God's people, spoke of a coming invasion by Assyria that represented God's judgment against Israel, and then announced divine restoration, which would follow when God's people made the appropriate changes.

> *"In that day I will restore*
> *David's fallen shelter—*
> *I will repair its broken walls*
> *and restore its ruins—*
> *and will rebuild it as it used to be."*
> AMOS 9:11

Letters

The apostolic letters (or epistles) are the New Testament's counterpart to the Old Testament's prophetic books. These letters were written either by those taught directly by Jesus or by students of those taught directly by Jesus. In the months and years following Christ's death and resurrection, the Christian Church expanded in all geographical directions. As it did, it ran up against new cultures and new ideologies, which led to new challenges and new questions. The letters were written to address those challenges and questions.

In contrast to the prophetic books of the Old Testament, the letters of the New Testament are composed of the kind of grammar we might use in our own correspondence—direct declarative sentences with limited use of poetry or other literary devices. In many cases we find a sense of urgency that calls for the message to get quickly and directly into the lives of God's people. But like the prophetic writers, the writers of the epistles often presume that the reader knows the circumstances that motivate the communication. Fortunately, we have the book of Acts available, in which we can find historical narrative reporting on the growth of the Christian Church. Also, as with reading the Law, we need to watch for clues that help us determine which principles are applicable for all time and which apply only to the local situation and the immediate cultural circumstances of the original readers of the letters.

A passage from Galatians will illustrate the point. This letter was written by the apostle Paul to a group of Christians in what today is southern Turkey, who had come to know Christ or learned more about Him during an earlier visit by Paul (see Acts 13:14–14:23). Though many came to believe in Jesus and celebrated the news that Paul brought, the gospel message was also met by verbal objection and physical mistreatment of the messengers. Paul wrote Galatians after his visit to the area because a subsequent group of teachers claiming a higher authority had contradicted his core message. In the letter Paul barely pauses for a civil greeting before lashing out at this new teaching: "I am astonished that you are so quickly deserting the one who called you to live in the grace of Christ and are turning to a different gospel—which is really no gospel at all. Evidently some people are throwing you into confusion and are trying to pervert the gospel of Christ" (Galatians 1:6–7). The remainder of the letter seeks to restore a proper understanding of the gospel, reaffirming the free and full forgiveness of sins offered by God through Jesus as a gift for everyone who believes. So, while it is a letter with an application targeted for a specific time and place, it also stands as a manifesto of the Christian gospel, which continues to inform and encourage us today.

Apocalyptic

Apocalyptic writing, the final genre of literature we will consider, may be the most challenging to read. Though the book of Revelation offers the most sustained use of this particular writing style, we find it in the Old Testament, as well, particularly in the second portion of Daniel. These inspired authors used this style of writing to address the future of the world, the fate of God's people in the face of attacks by those who oppose the Lord, the return of Jesus Christ to judge the world, and the nature of the eternal kingdom that Jesus will establish. What makes this type of literature more difficult to understand is the writing style, which paints the pages of our Bible with fantastic images and extended visual metaphors, all of which move against a brightly colored and surreal backdrop. Consider the following snapshot from Revelation 13:

> *Then I saw a second beast, coming out of the earth. It had two horns like a lamb, but it spoke like a dragon. It exercised all the authority of the first beast on its behalf, and made the earth and its inhabitants worship the first beast, whose fatal wound had been healed. And it performed great signs, even causing fire to come down from heaven to the earth in full view of the people. . . . It also forced all people, great and small, rich and poor, free and slave, to receive a mark on their right hands or on their foreheads, so that they could not buy or sell unless they had the mark, which is the name of the beast or the number of its name. This calls for wisdom. Let the person who has insight calculate the number of the beast, for it is the number of a man. That number is 666.*
> REVELATION 13:11–13, 16–18

What do the images represent? What do they teach us that can be applied to our lives as we manage our personal challenges and look toward tomorrow? Because these portions of scripture were often written against the backdrop of persecution, it is helpful to learn what we can about the historical circumstances that motivated the writing. Only with that background in view can we take on the task of correctly decoding the images. As intriguing as the apocalyptic literature can be, newcomers to reading the Bible should probably wait until they have become more seasoned in other portions of scripture before tackling these more challenging segments of

God's Word.

Within the confines of this longer chapter, we have been able to engage the topic of genre only at a fundamental level. But I trust you have become aware of its value. Though one page of the Bible can look very similar to the next, to best understand what God is saying to us in His Word, we must first determine how He is speaking.

Without context, effective communication can be hopelessly impaired. Consider the following story in that light:

> A young girl left home, rushing forward as quickly as her legs would carry her. After running for a short distance, she turned left, waving her arms wildly. She turned sharply to the left and then dodged left again. Approaching home, her eyes grew big as she came face-to-face with a woman wearing a dark mask.

It is highly unlikely that the vocabulary or the grammar used in telling this brief story prove to be an obstacle to understanding. Nevertheless, you may be unable to make much sense of the story until it is put in context. These sentences describe the scene at my daughter's softball game after she hit a fly ball to deep center field.

What is going on? Sometimes our struggle to understand a portion of the Bible or our failure to fully grasp what a biblical author is saying, relates to the fact that we lack details from the historical context. In this chapter we will explore this obstacle to understanding, offer a pathway to overcome it, and illustrate how a greater understanding of historical context can deepen our engagement with the message in God's Word.

The Obstacle

There is always more going on behind the scenes in the biblical world than the authors of the Bible directly report to us. In some ways this is a good thing. Too much information can overwhelm us and distract from the important points. If all the details of an event were included in every Bible story, we would soon find ourselves drowning in those details and struggling to trace the contours of the plot. Likewise, if more context details were added to a piece of poetry, it would defeat the simple elegance of the poet's presentation. Nevertheless, we find many instances in which background knowledge related to the political, social, or economic circumstances surrounding a set of verses is assumed by the biblical author. Without sufficient information, our understanding of a poetic verse or a Bible story can be dramatically impaired.

The death of King Josiah provides a helpful example. This ruler of God's people inherited a kingdom that had wandered far and wide from God's plan for the nation of Israel. As a reforming king, Josiah worked aggressively and tirelessly to repair the temple and to reanimate holy living among his subjects. This earned him a remarkable accolade from God: "Neither before nor after Josiah was there a king like him who turned to the Lord as he did—with all his heart and with all his soul and with all his strength, in accordance with all the Law of Moses" (2 Kings 23:25). The account of Josiah's death is not merely noted in scripture, but is punctuated by the tragic circumstances that surrounded it. At age thirty-nine, with so much more to offer, King Josiah picked an unnecessary fight with Necho, an Egyptian king, and died in battle.

Even though Josiah's death is recorded in two books of the

Bible (2 Kings 23:29–30 and 2 Chronicles 35:20–24), his death notice comes unexpectedly and we struggle to fully grasp what happened. Why was Necho marching north to Carchemish to engage in a battle on the side of the Assyrians? Why did Josiah engage in such a high-stakes venture, marching out against a much larger Egyptian army when the Egyptians had made it clear that their fight was not with Israel? Without answers to these questions, Bible readers cannot fully understand the death of this very important biblical figure, and we're left a bit uncertain about what lessons to draw from it.

The Solution

The solution to this challenge involves learning more about historical context. Though this may require us to leave the pages of the Bible; it does not require us to leave the story of God's interaction with the world. That's because all history, whether recorded in the Bible or not, is part of "His story." The God of the Bible is not just aware of history; He directs it. He makes history happen the way it does in order to accomplish the goals He has in mind for the world.

> *"Remember the former things, those of long ago; I am God, and there is no other; I am God, and there is none like me. I make known the end from the beginning, from ancient times, what is still to come. I say: 'My purpose will stand, and I will do all that I please.' From the east I summon a bird of prey; from a far-off land, a man to fulfill my purpose. What I have said, that I will bring about; what I have planned, that I will do."*
> ISAIAH 46:9–11

History is driven by God's divine purpose. Though His purpose is opposed by unseen spiritual forces (see Daniel 10:12–13), history happens as God intends. This includes everything from the massive to the mundane, from the building of a reservoir (see Isaiah 22:11) to the defeat of an empire that is blocking the advance of the divine kingdom (see Isaiah 37:26). In some cases this divine plan for history is articulated in great detail, as in Daniel 7–12. But in most cases Bible readers must turn to other resources in order to collect the necessary background information unreported in the Bible. Even if history not recorded in the Bible has an important connection to the divine plan, God is either formally sponsoring the action or tolerating the events that combine to accomplish the larger goals He has in mind.

As Bible readers we can make good use of historical background information from extrabiblical sources. Ancient historians and artists collected information of past events and preserved it in their artwork and written reports. Sometimes these reports and other artifacts are nearly contemporary with the events mentioned in the Bible. Other historical records associated with biblical events date to later centuries, but all earlier than the modern era. Of course none of this information was recorded by divine inspiration, so we do not grant these sources the same level of authority as reporting found in the Bible. Nevertheless, these extrabiblical accounts reveal God's work in the world and offer valuable historical background that can improve our understanding of what the Bible says.

Illustrations

The Death of King Josiah

Let's consider two narratives, one from the Old Testament and one from the New Testament, that illustrate the value of asking and answering the question, "What is going on behind the scenes?" The first story is one I've already mentioned—the untimely death of King Josiah. To understand what happens, we need to start with the big picture. Throughout much of the Old Testament, three national superpowers—Egypt, Assyria, and Babylon—cast their shadows over events and are mentioned frequently by the biblical authors. During the thousands of years encompassed by the Old Testament, these three nations experienced times of great national strength as well as times of economic and military weakness. They also contended among themselves to control the wealth and natural resources of territories outside their borders, including the strategic, natural land bridge inhabited by the Israelites.

The story of Josiah's death occurs late in the seventh century BC as an important change was occurring on the world's stage. The Assyrians, who had built an empire from the Persian Gulf to the Red Sea, were in a state of steady decline, slowly collapsing under pressure from the rising tide of the Neo-Babylonian Empire. With their heartland and capital city lost, the Assyrians were making one last bold stand near the city of Carchemish on the Euphrates River.

As Pharaoh Necho of Egypt and King Josiah of Judah sized up the situation, they perceived these evolving events differently. The Egyptians were pleased to have the Assyrians and Babylonians fighting each other to the point of physical and economic exhaustion. This opened the door for Egypt to fill the vacuum created when these two competitors had weakened one another. When Necho saw that Assyria was increasingly on the ropes, he developed a plan to prop up the flagging Assyrians by rolling Egyptian soldiers toward Carchemish. Josiah, meanwhile, had a different perspective. God's people, who had experienced a violent invasion and occupation of their land at the hands of Assyria, were happy to see the weakened empire on the brink of collapse. The other regional power, Babylon, was much farther east than Assyria, and Josiah may have hoped that the Babylonians would not seek to exert their influence over Israel, at least in the near future.

These details, gleaned from extrabiblical sources, help us understand why Necho was marching north to Carchemish to engage in a battle on the side of the Assyrians. His goal was to pass quickly through the territory of Judah on his way to assist the Assyrians at Carchemish, so that the Egyptians might take advantage of continuing hostilities between Assyria and Babylon. Why then did Josiah engage in such a high-stakes venture, marching out against the Egyptian army, when Necho had made it clear to him that Egypt's fight was not with Judah? Josiah's goal was to interrupt and delay the arrival of the Egyptian reinforcements so that Babylon might finish off the last vestiges of the Assyrian military resistance at Carchemish. In doing so he believed that his own kingdom would be preserved.

Understanding the historical background and the general role that God plays in history allows us to get the point of this brief narrative. It is not just that Josiah died, but that he died as a consequence of making a grave theological error. Despite his remarkable record of reformation and drawing the people of Judah back to God, Josiah's actions now put him in conflict with God's purposes. The Lord had planned for the Babylonians to defeat the Assyrians at Carchemish. He had also allowed for Egyptian involvement in this battle, though their presence would not change the outcome. Even though Necho had made his plans clear to Josiah (see 2 Chronicles 35:21), Josiah chose to rely on his own perception and his ability to manipulate world events. The story offers a stunning warning to everyone tempted to follow Josiah's lead. "He [Josiah] would not listen to what Necho had said at God's command but went to fight him on the plain of Megiddo" (2 Chronicles 35:22). No matter how well intentioned we might be, we cannot change God's plans, only live within them. Josiah paid for his act of hubris with his life.

The Verdict of Pontius Pilate

A second story that illustrates the value of historical background comes from the New Testament. It is the story of how the Jewish religious leaders manipulated Pontius Pilate, the Roman governor at the time of Jesus' arrest and trial. The interaction between the Jewish leaders, Jesus, and Pilate are recorded in all four Gospels (see Matthew 27:11–26; Mark 15:2–15; Luke 23:1–25; and John 18:29–19:16). But despite the attention paid by the biblical writers to these events, we are still missing a key piece of information that would allow us to answer an important question: Why did Pilate, the man holding the most powerful political position in the story, succumb to the pressure of the Jewish leaders and ultimately condemn an innocent man to die?

When Jesus confronted the local religious establishment of His day, whose leaders had been thoroughly corrupted, He picked a fight with a group of men who had a lot to lose and who were experienced in fighting for position and power. The aristocratic priests of Jerusalem stood to lose professionally, socially, and economically under Jesus' unrelenting criticism of their character and behavior. What is more, these wealthy politicians had been hardened by their negotiations with Rome and were of no mind to concede a single point to the upstart teacher from Galilee. They wanted to be rid of Jesus, but they did not want to dirty their own hands with the deed, so they set about executing a plan that would involve the Roman governor, Pontius Pilate. The charges the Jewish leaders brought against Jesus were serious. They claimed He was leading a movement to overthrow the Roman occupation of Judea. However, during Jesus' trial the charges collapsed in the face of the evidence, and Pilate appropriately pronounced Jesus' innocence. That is how the story should have ended; so why did the powerful governor yield to pressure as he did?

The answer lies both in Pilate's position and the political realities that undercut him. During the time of Jesus, the nation of Israel was under the control of Rome. This included the region of Judea and the city of Jerusalem. The man in charge of collecting the taxes and keeping the peace in that part of the Roman world was the Roman-appointed governor, Pontius Pilate. He was neither the first nor the last such governor, but he was the man in charge during the final years of Jesus' life on earth. Pilate's duties included those we associate with the executive branch of government, but they also extended into the judicial realm. He was, in effect, the Supreme Court justice. In the absence of a jury, he entertained the charges, heard the evidence, and issued the verdict. What is more, the only one empowered to overturn his verdict was the Roman emperor himself. During Jesus' trial, when Jesus did not immediately respond to the questions directed His way by Pilate, the Roman judge said, "Don't you realize I have power either to free you or to crucify you?" (John 19:10).

In many ways, Pilate had it right—which makes it all the more surprising to see justice go so horribly wrong when the Jewish leaders manipulate him into issuing a verdict he does not really own. But here is the background information that allows us to make more sense of these events. Pilate had come into office in AD 26, the fifth Roman governor over Judea since AD 6. His tenure in office was marked repeatedly by insensitivity to the cultures that he governed and by heartless cruelty against those he ruled. Josephus, the first-century historian, makes note of a number of such instances. For example, Pilate confiscated money from the temple treasury to pay for a new water-delivery system he was building for Jerusalem. And the Bible itself recalls an instance in which Pilate massacred Galileans who had come to worship at the temple in Jerusalem (see Luke 13:1–2).

Because Rome was far away from Judea, as long as the news of these abuses remained a local story, Pilate was unconcerned. But there was one thing that struck fear into the governor's heart: the prospect of Jewish citizens traveling to Rome to deliver a personal report on Pilate's misconduct. Here the Jewish historian Philo offers a crucial insight: "It was this final point which particularly exasperated him [Pilate], for he feared that if they actually sent an embassy, they would also expose the rest of his conduct as governor by stating in full the briberies, the insults, the robberies, the outrages and wanton injuries, the executions without trial constantly repeated, the ceaseless and supremely grievous cruelty" (Philo, *Embassy of Gauis*, paragraph 38). In the end, after the death and resurrection of Jesus, it was just this kind of report, delivered by the Samaritans, that resulted in Pilate's being recalled to Rome.

The Jewish leaders were well aware of Pilate's vulnerabilities and were quick to exploit them. When they sought to involve the governor in condemning Jesus, they played heavily on that fear to manipulate the verdict. At times the threat to send an embassy to report on Pilate was subtle, and at other times it was made very public—particularly when they were afraid that Pilate was about to release Jesus. They shouted as one, "If you let this man go, you are no friend of Caesar. Anyone who claims to be a king opposes Caesar" (John 19:12). The Jewish leaders put their finger on the one thing Pilate feared, and that is how they were able to manipulate this powerful Roman governor into issuing the desired verdict against Jesus.

Without context, effective communication is often hopelessly impaired. To deepen our understanding of God's Word, we can legitimately ask, "What is going on behind the scenes?" As we work to answer that question, we honor the fact that all history is part of God's story, and we tap in to a storehouse of information that provides essential background for understanding God's Word.

People of every age and location have unique cultural practices that leave outsiders scratching their heads and asking, "What are they doing?" Milwaukee, Wisconsin, is no exception. If you come to this city's beaches on January 1, you will see what I mean. Each year on this date, hundreds of people mill about on the Lake Michigan shoreline dressed in a wide variety of attire, from traditional swimwear to Green Bay Packers uniforms to three-piece business suits. Around noon this diverse group heads as one for the water. Some walk, most run, and a few daring souls ride their bikes toward the waves. No matter how they get there, the goal is the same: to take the first swim of the year in Lake Michigan. What is shocking is to realize that the water temperature is around 38 degrees and the outside air temperature might be in the teens—not counting windchill. The event is aptly named the Polar Bear Plunge.

There is no swimming in freezing water in the Bible, but as Bible readers we are certain to encounter cultural practices from the past that may amuse us and confuse us. In this chapter we will consider this category of misunderstanding, discuss how the mystery can be removed, and illustrate how a deeper understanding of ancient culture can advance our understanding of God's Word.

The Obstacle

What are they doing? Because the Bible was written by people living in the past about people who were going about the normal routines of daily life in that era and location, we can expect to encounter ancient cultural practices in our Bible reading. On the one hand, many of the day-to-day activities mentioned in the Bible strike a familiar chord. The human experience is the human experience, whether we lived two thousand years before the time of Christ or in the twenty-first century of the modern era. In a typical week, people everywhere do similar sorts of things—make and wear clothing, build and occupy homes, secure a supply of fresh water, and provide their families with food. People everywhere go to work, travel, and relax. These points of continuity in the human experience help us connect with cultures across the world and throughout history.

The challenge comes when we read about cultural practices that are foreign to our experience. For example, when we want a drink of water, we walk to the kitchen faucet or the refrigerator. In the ancient world, however, the story was very different. A drink of water came from a well or a cistern, which was dug by members of the family. Maintenance and defense of this water resource was a constant concern and occupied hours of time in any given week.

The same differences are apparent when we think about the bread we use to make our lunches. For most of us, bread comes from the local grocery store. In the ancient world, enjoying daily bread was the end of a yearlong process that involved plowing fields, planting, weeding, harvesting the grain, processing the grain into flour, and baking the bread for daily use.

In the Bible we often find unique cultural practices mentioned in narrative accounts. For example, the digging and defending of a well is at center stage in an episode from Abraham's life. A well that Abraham had dug at Beersheba is seized by a neighboring clan. Confrontation, negotiation, and a treaty ceremony become part of Abraham's story as this water rights issue is addressed (see Genesis 21:25–31). In the New Testament, a Samaritan village well becomes the centerpiece of a story from Jesus' life as He engages a woman from the village of Sychar in a conversation about water that turns into a conversation about His identity as the Messiah (see John 4:4–9).

We also find cultural practices used as metaphors in the Bible. For example, God's criticism of His chosen people is packaged in image-laden language: "My people have committed two sins: They have forsaken me, the spring of living water, and have dug their own cisterns, broken cisterns that cannot hold water" (Jeremiah 2:13). In the New Testament, Jesus cautions His disciples about becoming lax in their life's witness by employing the image of salt: "Salt is good, but if it loses its saltiness, how can it be made salty again? It is fit neither for the soil nor for the manure pile; it is thrown out. Whoever has ears to hear, let them hear" (Luke 14:34-36). We have ears with which to hear, but we do not have manure piles into which we throw salt! So we are left to ask, "What is going on here?" When cultural images foreign to our experience are introduced by the biblical writers, they can become obstacles to understanding.

The Solution

It can be more than a little difficult to keep up with the contemporary twists and turns of our own culture. We are met by a growing list of changes to master, whether that is new software on our computer, a new car that parallel parks itself, or a cell phone that acts more like a computer than a phone. That is to say nothing of the clothing and diet fads that seem to change weekly in our world. There is plenty of work to do in keeping up with our own changing culture without adding the burden of learning about ancient cultures. But for Bible readers the extra energy expended is worth the effort.

In light of the many recent discoveries in archaeology, it is now possible to immerse ourselves in a deeper understanding of ancient culture. Scholars continue to unearth fresh and exciting insights into the cultures of the past. Today we know more than ever about past practices such as betrothal and marriage, agriculture, and warfare. We also know more about the tools of ancient culture, such as grain mills, city gates, and olive presses. When we carry these insights into our study of the Bible, we will see things we had not seen before and will understand passages that once left us confused. The following illustrations demonstrate the value of cultural insight in our pursuit of deeper biblical understanding.

Illustrations

We can illustrate the value of becoming more culturally aware by briefly discussing ancient practices associated with cisterns, signet rings, betrothal, mangers, and salt.

Cistern

Israel is a land with precious few natural resources and a real shortage of freshwater. With the scarcity of freshwater lakes or rivers in the region, the freshwater used by those living in the Promised Land during Bible times was well water and rainwater. Gathering rainwater was relatively easy during the rainy months, but during the five months of the year when little or no rain fell, it was necessary to tap in to the supply of rainwater that had fallen weeks or months earlier. One way to do this was with a cistern, which in ancient Israel was an underground water-storage chamber dug into the limestone and plastered annually to keep it from leaking. On rainy days the surface runoff was directed into the cisterns, which varied in size depending on whether they were meeting the needs of a city or a single household. In cross-section, most cisterns have a bell-like shape with a narrow neck that connects the storage chamber with the earth's surface. The water entered the cistern and was drawn from the cistern through that neck.

The Bible mentions cisterns on several occasions. Some of these are associated with cities; others were dug in the country-side to provide water for grazing livestock (see 2 Chronicles 26:10). The unique design of a cistern made it an ideal place to imprison someone you wanted to detain. When Joseph's brothers chose to keep him in custody while determining his fate, they put him in a cistern (see Genesis 37.21–24). And those who found the prophet Jeremiah's message unwelcome detained him the same way (see Jeremiah 38:6).

Ironically, the book that bears Jeremiah's name employs the cistern as a metaphor to describe the poor choices that God's people had made. In spite of the constant care God had shown the Israelites, they had repeatedly violated the first commandment, turning their backs on the Lord while investing themselves in the worship of other gods. This behavior was so unthinkable it required illustration: "My people have committed two sins: They have forsaken me, the spring of living water, and have dug their own cisterns, broken cisterns that cannot hold water" (Jeremiah 2:13). To understand the metaphor, we need to understand the difference between water obtained from a spring and water obtained from a cistern; both are supplied by rainwater, but in very different ways. Rain absorbed by the soil trickles down to the water table. In most places, the water table is below the surface of the ground; but when the water table and ground level coincide in elevation, a spring breaks out, providing the most desirable water in the ancient world. Such springs did not require excavation or maintenance. What is more, the springwater was naturally filtered and always fresh. By contrast, water from a cistern was not naturally filtered and often brackish. On top of that, maintaining a cistern was time-and labor-intensive. First there was the initial excavation, but then the cistern required regular maintenance, as well—draining, cleaning, and replastering at least once a year. Without the necessary maintenance, the cistern would leak, resulting in a loss of water. In using the metaphor of springs and cisterns in Jeremiah 2:13, the Lord assumes the people are aware of the differences between the two. He compares Himself to the highly desirable springwater that Israel had abandoned. Instead, they had turned to other deities, who are likened not just to a cistern but to a broken cistern, which is incapable of holding water. The metaphor highlights the unthinkable nature of their actions.

Signet Ring

Better understanding of the signet ring can also deepen our understanding of God's message in the Bible. As the name suggests, the signet ring is a loop of metal, often stirruplike in shape with a flat upper surface. That upper surface is incised with a distinctive design, which, when pressed into soft clay or warmed wax, leaves a unique impression. A signet ring was unique to an individual, and the impression was used to mark a document as one's own, like putting a signature on an official document today.

We find both literal and figurative uses of signet rings in the Bible. For example, when Joseph rose in social rank from slave and prisoner to second in command of all Egypt, "Pharaoh took his signet ring from his finger and put it on Joseph's finger" (Genesis 41:42). Consider the power this gave Joseph; he now had the ability to execute the "signature" of the Egyptian ruler.

Because the signet ring was such a cherished personal possession, and because it carried the connotations of power, God uses it as a metaphor in referring to mortals who are leaders of His people. In the case of one king of Judah, the Lord expressed His displeasure over this man's leadership with these words: " 'As surely as I live,' declares the Lord, 'even if you, Jehoiachin son of Jehoiakim king of Judah, were a signet ring on my right hand, I would still pull you off' " (Jeremiah 22:24). On the other hand, the leadership of a subsequent descendant of David's is affirmed with exactly the opposite image: " 'On that day,' declares the Lord Almighty, 'I will take you, my servant Zerubbabel son of Shealtiel,' declares the Lord, 'and I will make you like my signet ring, for I have chosen you,' declares the LORD Almighty" (Haggai 2:23).

Betrothal

In American culture a ring plays a central role in a couple's engagement. Not so in the biblical world. In fact, many aspects of getting married in Israel during the first century are strikingly different from our modern experience. In a remote Jewish village like Nazareth, marriages were arranged—meaning it was the parents who identified the most desirable match for their sons and daughters, and then they made a marriage contract with the other family. Once that contract was made, the betrothal was on. It is not just the process of betrothal that sounds peculiar, but also the age of the betrothed. Evidence suggests that Jewish girls of the first century were engaged to be married when they were as young as eleven or twelve, and married by the time they were thirteen.

This information can really change our perspective on Mary, the mother of Jesus. In Luke 1 we read that an angel appeared to her to announce that she was going to have a remarkable experience. The long-awaited Savior was going to enter the mortal world via her body. This child would not be the biological child of her fiancé, Joseph, but rather, she was told, "The Holy Spirit will come on you, and the power of the Most High will overshadow you. So the holy one to be born will be called the Son of God" (Luke 1:35). Soon afterward, Mary expressed her willingness to take on this responsibility, laden with challenges as it was. She now would have to defend the legitimacy of this unique pregnancy to her fiancé, her family, and her neighbors. The angel presented an assignment that would have been a challenge for any seasoned adult, given the very conservative culture in Nazareth, let alone for a girl of eleven or twelve years. With this additional knowledge, we grow in appreciation of Mary's remarkable faith and character.

Manger

Mary was not much older than twelve or thirteen when she gave birth to Jesus and placed him in a manger. All ordinary families of Jesus' day had their own animals to provide the family with meat, milk, and shelter, as well as the capacity to carry heavy loads, pull plows, and draw wagons. During daylight hours, it was relatively safe for the animals to be in the open country. But at night, when large predators roamed the fields, the animals were brought into the family living compound for safekeeping. The food they ate was placed in a feedbox or manger. Such mangers were about as functional in material and design as they could be. A typical manger was about three feet long and three feet tall. It could be carved out of limestone, or more often, shaped out of compacted mud and clay. Of all the places in the ancient world we might look for decoration and elegance, this was not it. The ordinary manger was simple in form, utilitarian, and undecorated.

You may know that Jesus was placed in a manger shortly after His birth. But did you know that this fact is mentioned again and again for the sake of emphasis in the Christmas story? It is mentioned three times in the account of Jesus' birth (see Luke 2:7, 12, 16). And the manger is identified as a "sign" when the angel speaks to the Christmas shepherds. "This will be a sign to you: You will find a baby wrapped in cloths and lying in a manger" (Luke 2:12). For Luke a "sign" is always an image that carries special meaning. An animal feeding trough was no place for a baby, much less a baby who had been identified as royalty, much less the anticipated King of the world who would rule an eternal kingdom. The manger is emphasized in Luke because it offers an insight into how this divine King would rule. He would not rule the world with the arrogance displayed by so many mortal kings. This would be a humble king. And long before we hear Jesus say it, the manger sends the following message: "The Son of Man did not come to be served, but to serve, and to give his life as a ransom for many" (Matthew 20:28).

Salt

Salt is something we know about. We enjoy putting at least a pinch of salt on our food to improve its flavor. Those living in the days of Jesus did the same thing. However. the ancients would not have recognized the small white grains of nearly pure sodium chloride found in our saltshakers. For those living in Bible times, salt came to the table in chunks; and those chunks were anything but pure salt. A chunk of salt used to season food was actually composed of pure salt, soil, and other impurities that either lacked taste or carried a bitter taste. To get some of the more desirable salt from that chunk, it was necessary to pound it on the table or floor to flake off some of the pure salt. Over time this process would leave a person with a chunk of material that contained a whole lot more by-product than salt—salt that had lost its saltiness, if you will. A chunk of salt in this condition was no longer valuable for seasoning food, nor was it worth throwing into the family manure pile.

That last point requires some explanation. People in Bible times had to build fires both for cooking meals and for keeping warm during the colder winter months. Because there was a shortage of timber in the Promised Land, those fires were most often kindled with grasses, brush, and manure. Families gathered the manure left behind by their animals, moistened it, and added salt. Because this salted manure burned at a higher temperature, it produced a more efficient fire for cooking a meal or heating a home.

Jesus seized upon this imagery when discussing the important role His disciples were to play in the world. The message of Jesus had changed them so that they, in turn, might begin to change the lives of those around them. In this way, they had become like salt, capable of improving those whose lives they touched. However, if they retreated from the teachings of Jesus or failed to enact them in their lives, that positive influence would be lost. Jesus conveyed this message with salt imagery. "Salt is good, but if it loses its saltiness, how can it be made salty again? It is fit neither for the soil nor for the manure pile; it is thrown out" (Luke 14:34–35).

As we have seen, it is possible to understand the culture of the biblical world and learn more about the implements and practices we find in the pages of our Bibles. New and deeper understanding is sure to follow when we ask and answer the question, "What are they doing?"

Whenever we leave home to explore less familiar places, getting lost is bound to happen. It's part of learning our way around—even if we have maps or an onboard GPS. Sometimes, asking for directions is the only hope we have. But asking directions from a local offers no guarantee that we won't end up feeling even more lost. Have you ever gotten directions that sounded something like this? "All you need to do is turn south at the next intersection. Keep going until you get to the farm that Sam Jenkins gave to his grandson two years ago, and then turn east. From there it is just four miles the other side of Miller Lake. You can't miss it!" When the biblical authors start to mention geography, it can sound just about as impenetrable and confusing as that. For example, you might be familiar with the story of David and Goliath, but what are we to make of the two verses that start this familiar story? "Now the Philistines gathered their forces for war and assembled at Sokoh in Judah. They pitched camp at Ephes Dammim, between Sokoh and Azekah. Saul and the Israelites assembled and camped in the Valley of Elah" (1 Samuel 17:1–2).

Where am I? Open to just about any page in the Bible and you will find at least a few references to geography. Sometimes it will be the name of a city or region. Other times it will be a reference to terrain or rainfall. And still other pages, such as those in the latter half of Joshua, will be filled with nothing but long lists of place names that sound as peculiar to us as the street names in our local community would have sounded to someone living in Joshua's day. If we do not ignore these lists altogether, our best efforts to negotiate them can leave us exhausted and frustrated. The goal of this chapter is to take the geographical obstacle out of the way. It will help you understand why geography appears so frequently in the pages of the Bible. We will discuss how we might come to a better understanding of biblical geography and illustrate the insights we can obtain when we bring a better understanding of biblical geography to our Bible reading.

The Obstacle

Geography appears often on the pages of the Bible for three reasons. First, the Bible is filled with stories about real people who lived in real places. Knowing something about the places these people lived can help us understand more about lives and circumstances. Next, we encounter geography in our Bible reading because God has intimately linked the central message of the Bible to a place, the Promised Land. In reading the Bible, we get no further than Genesis 12 before that connection becomes clear. Although God's creation had rebelled against Him, He was not about to abandon it. The biggest of the big ideas in the Bible is that God would send a Savior to rescue the world from its sin-ruined state. When God connected that promise to the family of Abram, He also connected it to Canaan, the Promised Land. In time the Messiah came from Abram's descendants and accomplished his saving mission in that same geographical location (see Genesis 3:1–3). From Genesis 3 on, the inspired authors of the Bible never let this detail stray far from their focus. The central message of the Bible is firmly linked to geography.

The third reason that geography finds its way so frequently

onto the pages of the Bible is that geography has the ability to influence our perceptions and responses. Consider the power of the phrase, "Remember the Alamo!" This cry, used at the battle of San Jacinto in 1836, employs a place name meant to encourage those fighting for the independence of Texas. It had the power to inspire because it was not just a place name, but a place name linked to a highly charged, emotional event. Places are not merely locations on a map; they carry connotations that the biblical authors can use to influence perception and call for action.

As the Holy Spirit guided the hands and hearts of the Bible's inspired authors, He frequently directed them to include mention of geography. Sometimes that geography appears in poetry: "As the mountains surround Jerusalem, so the LORD surrounds his people both now and forevermore" (Psalm 125:2). At other times, it appears in familiar Bible stories, such as the story of David and Goliath. In each case, whether subtle or striking, geography can become an obstacle to understanding, because we simply are not familiar with that part of the world.

The Solution

The first step in understanding how geography can aid our understanding of the Bible is to begin to notice when we run across geographical references. Of course, that means knowing what geography is. Perhaps the first thing that comes to mind is a map. But maps are only tools that display geography. So what is geography? To make it easy, think in terms of two categories: the features and processes that happen on the surface of the earth (physical geography) and the way in which humans respond to those features and processes (human geography). When I read a portion of the Bible, I pay attention to mentions of geology, topography, water, climate, and forestation. I also look for the cultural responses to that geography: water acquisition, city and home construction, land use, and road building. Again, the first step is to notice those details as you read.

The second step is to learn as much as we can about the geographical items we encounter. The proper names of places like the Elah Valley, Sokoh, Shechem, or even Jerusalem will require us to become spatially oriented. A helpful place to start is with a Bible atlas, which can provide basic information on the lands of the Bible and maps to assist in your orientation. Other books written about the physical and human geography of the biblical world can help us learn more about these dimensions of the Bible. The illustrations that follow will demonstrate the value of taking such tools in hand as we read.

Illustration

The Story of David and Goliath

The story of David and Goliath begins with a rush of geographical details that most people fail to notice. "Now the Philistines gathered their forces for war and assembled at Sokoh in Judah. They pitched camp at Ephes Dammim, between Sokoh and Azekah. Saul and the Israelites assembled and camped in the Valley of Elah and drew up their battle line to meet the Philistines" (1 Samuel 17:1–2). We will do a bit of work to decode this geographical description before we consider the ways in which understanding the geography changes our reading of the narrative.

In the first verses of the story, the inspired author directs our attention to the Elah Valley; all the other place names (Sokoh, Azekah, Ephes Dammim) have a connection to this valley. To understand the importance of the Elah Valley is to understand the connection between geography and national security in ancient Israel. The western portion of the Promised Land that runs along the Mediterranean Sea is an undulating plain that gently rises and falls with less than 150 feet of elevation change. This is where the Philistines lived, on the agriculturally rich and open coastal plain. By contrast the Israelites lived along the mountain spine that runs north and south through the heart of Israel. The hilly terrain of central Israel is difficult to farm, but it offers a great deal of security. Between the mountainous region where the Israelites lived and the coastal plain where the Philistines lived is a transition zone called the Shephelah. The Shephelah region is characterized by lower foothills and wide valleys. The valleys run east and west, perpendicular to the mountains, providing a natural travel corridor from the coastal plain to the mountainous interior. To enjoy the highest level of national security, the Israelites needed to control these valleys as a buffer zone. If their chief rival, the Philistines, elected to attack, they would do so using a valley in the Shephelah. If the Israelites lost the battle in the valley, it put their homes, cities, and villages in imminent danger.

That general picture will help us decode what the author of 1 Samuel says about the circumstances on the day that David defeated Goliath. The Philistines had pitched their camp in one of the Shephelah valleys called the Elah Valley. The position of their camp is given in some detail. They were camped in Ephes Dammim between Sokoh and Azekah. This means that the Philistines had not just entered the Elah Valley but had penetrated and now controlled nearly the entire extent of it. This left King Saul and his soldiers clinging to the far eastern section of this critical valley, which had been all but lost to the Philistine invaders.

How does the geography of 1 Samuel 17:1–3 shape the way we read the story of David and Goliath? Consider first what this story is about. God had selected Saul to be the first king of Israel. His role as king was clearly defined both by his subjects and by God. His subjects expected Saul to go before them and fight their battles (see 1 Samuel 8:20). The Lord had made it clear that Israel's king was to lead the people so that they might remain faithful to God and accomplish the sacred mission of bringing the Messiah into the world (see Deuteronomy 17:14–20). Sadly, Saul failed on both counts. That is why the Lord anointed David as the king who would succeed Saul (see 1 Samuel 16).

Those details, when combined with an understanding of the geography, set the stage for the story of David and Goliath. On the one hand, political tension fills the air. Saul, the sitting king, has been rejected by God. Yet the newly anointed king has not been publicly recognized or sworn into office. The political tension is driven by the question of who is to lead God's people. The geographical information given in the introduction to this story indicates that Israel is witnessing a full-blown national emergency. The Philistines have marched their armies deep into the Elah Valley and show no signs of stopping there. If there was a time for faith, if there was a time for courage, if there was a time for godly leadership, this was it.

With a political crisis and national emergency hanging in the air, we are invited to compare the ways in which Saul and David respond. Saul had failed to lead or inspire anything but fear in his men for more than a month (see 1 Samuel 17:11, 16). By contrast, David changes everything within a day of his arrival. With words and actions, he proves that he is the one with the robust faith in God and the courage that might bring security to Israel. Goliath bristled with the latest and greatest in military technology, but David had something more. "You come against me with sword and spear and javelin, but I come against you in the name of the LORD Almighty, the God of the armies of Israel, whom you have defied" (1 Samuel 17:45). In the Elah Valley, we see what we have come to expect from Saul: more weakness and failure. He does not leave the royal throne by the close of the narrative, but we leave the story even more convinced that his time is up and that David's time has come. Our impression of both leaders is informed by our understanding of the geographical location of the impending battle.

The Mountains
Surrounding Jerusalem

The poetry of the Old Testament lifts our eyes from the mundane to the magnificent, from the ordinary and upsetting circumstances of life to the enduring promises of God. Yet, in lifting our eyes to the heavens, these divinely inspired poets often turn our eyes back to the earth as they search for images to convey their message. That is the case in Psalm 125, where the psalmist challenges us to see how geography has something to teach us about the magnificence of the Lord.

> *Those who trust in the LORD*
> *are like Mount Zion,*
> *which cannot be shaken but endures forever.*
> *As the mountains surround Jerusalem,*
> *so the LORD surrounds his people*
> *both now and forevermore.*
> PSALM 125:1–2

Again, let's extract and study the geography before we consider its role in these verses. The mention of Mount Zion and Jerusalem immediately takes us to the city that had become Israel's religious and political capital (see 2 Samuel 5:6–10). At first blush we may question the logic of David's choice of Jerusalem, because the city came with a load of unappealing baggage. David's Jerusalem had a meager water supply that would support a relatively small population. The narrow valleys that surround and bisect Jerusalem offer little by way of level ground for growing food. Furthermore, the city was located some distance away from the major transportation arteries that carried the commerce of the world, so there was very little money to be made here. But the one advantage that outweighed all the negatives was security.

The security of Jerusalem has a direct link to the topography of the region. Jerusalem is buried deep in the central mountains of Israel, miles from the flat and accessible coastal plain that runs north and south along the Mediterranean Sea. International armies with a mind to attack and defeat Jerusalem had quite a task before them. After arriving on the more easily traveled coastal plain, they soon found themselves picking their way east through difficult, mountainous terrain. Some routes through the mountains proved more promising travel corridors than others, but in most cases, invading armies were confronted by narrow V-shaped valleys, which put the invading soldiers in a constricted setting where fatal blows could be struck from above. The less numerous and less well-equipped Israelite soldiers were so effective at using this terrain to their advantage that many international powers never made an attempt to reach the capital city. The rewards were too small and the risk was too high to make an assault on Jerusalem worthwhile. Because the mountains that surround Jerusalem also protected it, they became synonymous with the security of the capital city.

The second quality of these mountains that the poet puts to work is their endurance. The mountains surrounding Jerusalem look much the same today as they did three thousand years ago. In any one lifetime, they simply do not change. They owe their longevity to their geologic composition. These mountains are composed of Cenomanian limestone, the surface of which erodes at a rate of approximately one centimeter per thousand years! At that rate, those who walk the ridges and tend the valleys never see a significant change. From a human perspective, the mountains that surround Jerusalem do not change and thus appear poised to endure forever.

With that geography in mind, let's return to Psalm 125. This hymn of worship, along with other psalms labeled "A Song of Ascents," were traditionally used by Jewish pilgrims who were ascending the valleys leading up to Jerusalem. Their hearts and minds were set on worshipping the Lord at His temple. These songs accompanied their steps and challenged them to see life as God sees it. In the case of Psalm 125, the opening verses celebrate the benefits gleaned by those who put their trust in the Lord. They are like the place to which they are going to worship, Mount Zion. Though perils might threaten on the coast, the capital remains unshaken because the Lord has taken up a defensive position around His people. He is, in fact, like the mountains that reach out from and surround Jerusalem.

The security the Lord provides is not only sturdy and solid like the mountains, but it also endures like the mountains. The inspired poet reminds us not once but twice that God's people enjoy protection that endures forever. Though the mountains will change over the course of millennia, the Lord's promise of security never changes or expires. "As the mountains surround Jerusalem, so the LORD surrounds his people both now and forevermore" (Psalm 125:2).

Where am I? Open to just about any page in the Bible and you will find references to geography. Sometimes it will be the name of a city or region. Other times it will be a reference to terrain or rainfall. And there will be more than a few place names that sound as peculiar to us as the street names in our local community would have sounded to someone living in Jesus' day. Using the suggestions in this chapter, turn those quiet, unassuming, even confusing references into an opportunity to learn about the Bible's geography and how it shapes the Bible's message.

Do You Understand
What You Are Reading?

Although Philip, "the evangelist" of the Bible, initially directed this probing question to a well-educated man from Ethiopia, it is a question that confronts us as contemporary Bible readers, as well. The question acknowledges a reality that we know all too well: At times and in places, the Bible can be difficult to understand. So our desire to read God's Word lives in tension with the frustration we may feel when we do.

These frustrations often cause the most important book we could ever read to go unread. And as our Bibles sit on the shelf collecting dust, we do without the incredible insights and the enduring comfort God desperately wants to share with us.

Fortunately this dilemma has a solution—as this book has attempted to show, the major obstacles that stand in the way of our Bible reading can be diminished. When we appreciate the unique heritage of the Bible—its divine and human sides— we find it easier to engage when scripture challenges us to believe the unbelievable and to do the unthinkable. When we remember that while the Bible generally moves forward in time from the book of Genesis through the book of Revelation— but that it also circles back to repeat and emphasize "big ideas" that God longs to share with us—we'll be better able to follow the overall story line of scripture. When we observe changes in genre and put our minds in concert with those particular styles of writing, we will be rewarded with a more satisfying experience. And when we appreciate the historical, cultural, or geographical context of each passage, we find deepened insights into God's Word.

Do you understand what you are reading? We may never understand everything—but we will understand much more when we ask and answer the questions posed in this book: What is the Bible? What is God talking about? How is God speaking? What is going on behind the scenes? What are they doing? Where am I?

We pray that God will bless you as you follow these questions down the path to a deeper understanding of His Word.

With the principles of Understand Your Bible *in mind, why not try reading through your Bible in a year? The following plan divides scripture into Old Testament, New Testament, and wisdom book readings that will take you 15-20 minutes a day.*

A Plan for Reading
through the Bible
in a Year

☐ Day 1	Gen. 1–2	Matt. 1	Ps. 1
☐ Day 2	Gen. 3–4	Matt. 2	Ps. 2
☐ Day 3	Gen. 5–7	Matt. 3	Ps. 3
☐ Day 4	Gen. 8–10	Matt. 4	Ps. 4
☐ Day 5	Gen. 11–13	Matt. 5:1–20	Ps. 5
☐ Day 6	Gen. 14–16	Matt. 5:21–48	Ps. 6
☐ Day 7	Gen. 17–18	Matt. 6:1–18	Ps. 7
☐ Day 8	Gen. 19–20	Matt. 6:19–34	Ps. 8
☐ Day 9	Gen. 21–23	Matt. 7:1–11	Ps. 9:1–8
☐ Day 10	Gen. 24	Matt. 7:12–29	Ps. 9:9–20
☐ Day 11	Gen. 25–26	Matt. 8:1–17	Ps. 10:1–11
☐ Day 12	Gen. 27:1–28:9	Matt. 8:18–34	Ps. 10:12–18
☐ Day 13	Gen. 28:10–29:35	Matt. 9	Ps. 11
☐ Day 14	Gen. 30:1–31:21	Matt. 10:1–15	Ps. 12
☐ Day 15	Gen. 31:22–32:21	Matt. 10:16–36	Ps. 13
☐ Day 16	Gen. 32:22–34:31	Matt. 10:37–11:6	Ps. 14
☐ Day 17	Gen. 35–36	Matt. 11:7–24	Ps. 15
☐ Day 18	Gen. 37–38	Matt. 11:25–30	Ps. 16
☐ Day 19	Gen. 39–40	Matt. 12:1–29	Ps. 17
☐ Day 20	Gen. 41	Matt. 12:30–50	Ps. 18:1–15
☐ Day 21	Gen. 42–43	Matt. 13:1–9	Ps. 18:16–29
☐ Day 22	Gen. 44–45	Matt. 13:10–23	Ps. 18:30–50
☐ Day 23	Gen. 46:1–47:26	Matt. 13:24–43	Ps. 19
☐ Day 24	Gen. 47:27–49:28	Matt. 13:44–58	Ps. 20

☐ Day 25	Gen. 49:29–Exod. 1:22	Matt. 14	Ps. 21
☐ Day 26	Exod. 2–3	Matt. 15:1–28	Ps. 22:1–21
☐ Day 27	Exod. 4:1–5:21	Matt. 15:29–16:12	Ps. 22:22–31
☐ Day 28	Exod. 5:22–7:24	Matt. 16:13–28	Ps. 23
☐ Day 29	Exod. 7:25–9:35	Matt. 17:1–9	Ps. 24
☐ Day 30	Exod. 10–11	Matt. 17:10–27	Ps. 25
☐ Day 31	Exod. 12	Matt. 18:1–20	Ps. 26
☐ Day 32	Exod. 13–14	Matt. 18:21–35	Ps. 27
☐ Day 33	Exod. 15–16	Matt. 19:1–15	Ps. 28
☐ Day 34	Exod. 17–19	Matt. 19:16–30	Ps. 29
☐ Day 35	Exod. 20–21	Matt. 20:1–19	Ps. 30
☐ Day 36	Exod. 22–23	Matt. 20:20–34	Ps. 31:1–8
☐ Day 37	Exod. 24–25	Matt. 21:1–27	Ps. 31:9–18
☐ Day 38	Exod. 26–27	Matt. 21:28–46	Ps. 31:19–24
☐ Day 39	Exod. 28	Matt. 22	Ps. 32
☐ Day 40	Exod. 29	Matt. 23:1–36	Ps. 33:1–12
☐ Day 41	Exod. 30–31	Matt. 23:37–24:28	Ps. 33:13–22
☐ Day 42	Exod. 32–33	Matt. 24:29–51	Ps. 34:1–7
☐ Day 43	Exod. 34:1–35:29	Matt. 25:1–13	Ps. 34:8–22
☐ Day 44	Exod. 35:30–37:29	Matt. 25:14–30	Ps. 35:1–8
☐ Day 45	Exod. 38–39	Matt. 25:31–46	Ps. 35:9–17
☐ Day 46	Exod. 40	Matt. 26:1–35	Ps. 35:18–28
☐ Day 47	Lev. 1–3	Matt. 26:36–68	Ps. 36:1–6
☐ Day 48	Lev. 4:1–5:13	Matt. 26:69–27:26	Ps. 36:7–12

☐ Day 49	Lev. 5:14 -7:21	Matt. 27:27–50	Ps. 37:1–6
☐ Day 50	Lev. 7:22–8:36	Matt. 27:51–66	Ps. 37:7–26
☐ Day 51	Lev. 9–10	Matt. 28	Ps. 37:27–40
☐ Day 52	Lev. 11–12	Mark 1:1–28	Ps. 38
☐ Day 53	Lev. 13	Mark 1:29–39	Ps. 39
☐ Day 54	Lev. 14	Mark 1:40–2:12	Ps. 40:1–8
☐ Day 55	Lev. 15	Mark 2:13–3:35	Ps. 40:9–17
☐ Day 56	Lev. 16–17	Mark 4:1–20	Ps. 41:1–4
☐ Day 57	Lev. 18–19	Mark 4:21–41	Ps. 41:5–13
☐ Day 58	Lev. 20	Mark 5	Ps. 42–43
☐ Day 59	Lev. 21–22	Mark 6:1–13	Ps. 44
☐ Day 60	Lev. 23–24	Mark 6:14–29	Ps. 45:1–5
☐ Day 61	Lev. 25	Mark 6:30–56	Ps. 45:6–12
☐ Day 62	Lev. 26	Mark 7	Ps. 45:13–17
☐ Day 63	Lev. 27	Mark 8	Ps. 46
☐ Day 64	Num. 1–2	Mark 9:1–13	Ps. 47
☐ Day 65	Num. 3	Mark 9:14–50	Ps. 48:1–8
☐ Day 66	Num. 4	Mark 10:1–34	Ps. 48:9–14
☐ Day 67	Num. 5:1–6:21	Mark 10:35–52	Ps. 49:1–9
☐ Day 68	Num. 6:22–7:47	Mark 11	Ps. 49:10–20
☐ Day 69	Num. 7:48–8:4	Mark 12:1–27	Ps. 50:1–15
☐ Day 70	Num. 8:5–9:23	Mark 12:28–44	Ps. 50:16–23
☐ Day 71	Num. 10–11	Mark 13:1–8	Ps. 51:1–9
☐ Day 72	Num. 12–13	Mark 13:9–37	Ps. 51:10–19

☐ Day 73	Num. 14	Mark 14:1–31	Ps. 52
☐ Day 74	Num. 15	Mark 14:32–72	Ps. 53
☐ Day 75	Num. 16	Mark 15:1–32	Ps. 54
☐ Day 76	Num. 17–18	Mark 15:33–47	Ps. 55
☐ Day 77	Num. 19–20	Mark 16	Ps. 56:1–7
☐ Day 78	Num. 21:1–22:20	Luke 1:1–25	Ps. 56:8–13
☐ Day 79	Num. 22:21–23:30	Luke 1:26–56	Ps. 57
☐ Day 80	Num. 24–25	Luke 1:57–2:20	Ps. 58
☐ Day 81	Num. 26:1–27:11	Luke 2:21–38	Ps. 59:1–8
☐ Day 82	Num. 27:12–29:11	Luke 2:39–52	Ps. 59:9–17
☐ Day 83	Num. 29:12–30:16	Luke 3	Ps. 60:1–5
☐ Day 84	Num. 31	Luke 4	Ps. 60:6–12
☐ Day 85	Num. 32–33	Luke 5:1–16	Ps. 61
☐ Day 86	Num. 34–36	Luke 5:17–32	Ps. 62:1–6
☐ Day 87	Deut. 1:1–2:25	Luke 5:33–6:11	Ps. 62:7–12
☐ Day 88	Deut. 2:26–4:14	Luke 6:12–35	Ps. 63:1–5
☐ Day 89	Deut. 4:15–5:22	Luke 6:36–49	Ps. 63:6–11
☐ Day 90	Deut. 5:23–7:26	Luke 7:1–17	Ps. 64:1–5
☐ Day 91	Deut. 8–9	Luke 7:18–35	Ps. 64:6–10
☐ Day 92	Deut. 10–11	Luke 7:36–8:3	Ps. 65:1–8
☐ Day 93	Deut. 12–13	Luke 8:4–21	Ps. 65:9–13
☐ Day 94	Deut. 14:1–16:8	Luke 8:22–39	Ps. 66:1–7
☐ Day 95	Deut. 16:9–18:22	Luke 8:40–56	Ps. 66:8–15
☐ Day 96	Deut. 19:1–21:9	Luke 9:1–22	Ps. 66:16–20

☐ Day 97	Deut. 21:10–23:8	Luke 9:23–42	Ps. 67
☐ Day 98	Deut. 23:9–25:19	Luke 9:43–62	Ps. 68:1–6
☐ Day 99	Deut. 26:1–28:14	Luke 10:1–20	Ps. 68:7–14
☐ Day 100	Deut. 28:15–68	Luke 10:21–37	Ps. 68:15–19
☐ Day 101	Deut. 29–30	Luke 10:38–11:23	Ps. 68:20–27
☐ Day 102	Deut. 31:1–32:22	Luke 11:24–36	Ps. 68:28–35
☐ Day 103	Deut. 32:23–33:29	Luke 11:37–54	Ps. 69:1–9
☐ Day 104	Deut. 34–Josh. 2	Luke 12:1–15	Ps. 69:10–17
☐ Day 105	Josh. 3:1–5:12	Luke 12:16–40	Ps. 69:18–28
☐ Day 106	Josh. 5:13–7:26	Luke 12:41–48	Ps. 69:29–36
☐ Day 107	Josh. 8–9	Luke 12:49–59	Ps. 70
☐ Day 108	Josh. 10:1–11:15	Luke 13:1–21	Ps. 71:1–6
☐ Day 109	Josh. 11:16–13:33	Luke 13:22–35	Ps. 71:7–16
☐ Day 110	Josh. 14–16	Luke 14:1–15	Ps. 71:17–21
☐ Day 111	Josh. 17:1–19:16	Luke 14:16–35	Ps. 71:22–24
☐ Day 112	Josh. 19:17–21:42	Luke 15:1–10	Ps. 72:1–11
☐ Day 113	Josh. 21:43–22:34	Luke 15:11–32	Ps. 72:12–20
☐ Day 114	Josh. 23–24	Luke 16:1–18	Ps. 73:1–9
☐ Day 115	Judg. 1–2	Luke 16:19–17:10	Ps. 73:10–20
☐ Day 116	Judg. 3–4	Luke 17:11–37	Ps. 73:21–28
☐ Day 117	Judg. 5:1–6:24	Luke 18:1–17	Ps. 74:1–3
☐ Day 118	Judg. 6:25–7:25	Luke 18:18–43	Ps. 74:4–11
☐ Day 119	Judg. 8:1–9:23	Luke 19:1–28	Ps. 74:12–17
☐ Day 120	Judg. 9:24–10:18	Luke 19:29–48	Ps. 74:18–23

☐ Day 121	Judg. 11:1–12:7	Luke 20:1–26	Ps. 75:1–7
☐ Day 122	Judg. 12:8–14:20	Luke 20:27–47	Ps. 75:8–10
☐ Day 123	Judg. 15–16	Luke 21:1–19	Ps. 76:1–7
☐ Day 124	Judg. 17–18	Luke 21:20–22:6	Ps. 76:8–12
☐ Day 125	Judg. 19:1–20:23	Luke 22:7–30	Ps. 77:1–11
☐ Day 126	Judg. 20:24–21:25	Luke 22:31–54	Ps. 77:12–20
☐ Day 127	Ruth 1–2	Luke 22:55–23:25	Ps. 78:1–4
☐ Day 128	Ruth 3–4	Luke 23:26–24:12	Ps. 78:5–8
☐ Day 129	1 Sam. 1:1–2:21	Luke 24:13–53	Ps. 78:9–16
☐ Day 130	1 Sam. 2:22–4:22	John 1:1–28	Ps. 78:17–24
☐ Day 131	1 Sam. 5–7	John 1:29–51	Ps. 78:25–33
☐ Day 132	1 Sam. 8:1–9:26	John 2	Ps. 78:34–41
☐ Day 133	1 Sam. 9:27–11:15	John 3:1–22	Ps. 78:42–55
☐ Day 134	1 Sam. 12–13	John 3:23–4:10	Ps. 78:56–66
☐ Day 135	1 Sam. 14	John 4:11–38	Ps. 78:67–72
☐ Day 136	1 Sam. 15–16	John 4:39–54	Ps. 79:1–7
☐ Day 137	1 Sam. 17	John 5:1–24	Ps. 79:8–13
☐ Day 138	1 Sam. 18–19	John 5:25–47	Ps. 80:1–7
☐ Day 139	1 Sam. 20–21	John 6:1–21	Ps. 80:8–19
☐ Day 140	1 Sam. 22–23	John 6:22–42	Ps. 81:1–10
☐ Day 141	1 Sam. 24:1–25:31	John 6:43–71	Ps. 81:11–16
☐ Day 142	1 Sam. 25:32–27:12	John 7:1–24	Ps. 82
☐ Day 143	1 Sam. 28–29	John 7:25–8:11	Ps. 83
☐ Day 144	1 Sam. 30–31	John 8:12–47	Ps. 84:1–4

☐ Day 145	2 Sam. 1–2	John 8:48–9:12	Ps. 84:5–12
☐ Day 146	2 Sam. 3–4	John 9:13–34	Ps. 85:1–7
☐ Day 147	2 Sam. 5:1–7:17	John 9:35–10:10	Ps. 85:8–13
☐ Day 148	2 Sam. 7:18–10:19	John 10:11–30	Ps. 86:1–10
☐ Day 149	2 Sam. 11:1–12:25	John 10:31–11:16	Ps. 86:11–17
☐ Day 150	2 Sam. 12:26–13:39	John 11:17–54	Ps. 87
☐ Day 151	2 Sam. 14:1–15:12	John 11:55–12:19	Ps. 88:1–9
☐ Day 152	2 Sam. 15:13–16:23	John 12:20–43	Ps. 88:10–18
☐ Day 153	2 Sam. 17:1–18:18	John 12:44–13:20	Ps. 89:1–6
☐ Day 154	2 Sam. 18:19–19:39	John 13:21–38	Ps. 89:7–13
☐ Day 155	2 Sam. 19:40–21:22	John 14:1–17	Ps. 89:14–18
☐ Day 156	2 Sam. 22:1–23:7	John 14:18–15:27	Ps. 89:19–29
☐ Day 157	2 Sam. 23:8–24:25	John 16:1–22	Ps. 89:30–37
☐ Day 158	1 Kings 1	John 16:23–17:5	Ps. 89:38–52
☐ Day 159	1 Kings 2	John 17:6–26	Ps. 90:1–12
☐ Day 160	1 Kings 3–4	John 18:1–27	Ps. 90:13–17
☐ Day 161	1 Kings 5–6	John 18:28–19:5	Ps. 91:1–10
☐ Day 162	1 Kings 7	John 19:6–25a	Ps. 91:11–16
☐ Day 163	1 Kings 8:1–53	John 19:25b–42	Ps. 92:1–9
☐ Day 164	1 Kings 8:54–10:13	John 20:1–18	Ps. 92:10–15
☐ Day 165	1 Kings 10:14–11:43	John 20:19–31	Ps. 93
☐ Day 166	1 Kings 12:1–13:10	John 21	Ps. 94:1–11
☐ Day 167	1 Kings 13:11–14:31	Acts 1:1–11	Ps. 94:12–23
☐ Day 168	1 Kings 15:1–16:20	Acts 1:12–26	Ps. 95

☐ Day 169	1 Kings 16:21–18:19	Acts 2:1–21	Ps. 96:1–8
☐ Day 170	1 Kings 18:20–19:21	Acts2:22–41	Ps. 96:9–13
☐ Day 171	1 Kings 20	Acts 2:42–3:26	Ps. 97:1–6
☐ Day 172	1 Kings 21:1–22:28	Acts 4:1–22	Ps. 97:7–12
☐ Day 173	1 Kings 22:29–2 Kings 1:18	Acts 4:23–5:11	Ps. 98
☐ Day 174	2 Kings 2–3	Acts 5:12–28	Ps. 99
☐ Day 175	2 Kings 4	Acts 5:29–6:15	Ps. 100
☐ Day 176	2 Kings 5:1–6:23	Acts 7:1–16	Ps. 101
☐ Day 177	2 Kings 6:24–8:15	Acts 7:17–36	Ps. 102:1–7
☐ Day 178	2 Kings 8:16–9:37	Acts 7:37–53	Ps. 102:8–17
☐ Day 179	2 Kings 10–11	Acts 7:54–8:8	Ps. 102:18–28
☐ Day 180	2 Kings 12–13	Acts 8:9–40	Ps. 103:1–9
☐ Day 181	2 Kings 14–15	Acts 9:1–16	Ps. 103:10–14
☐ Day 182	2 Kings 16–17	Acts 9:17–31	Ps. 103:15–22
☐ Day 183	2 Kings 18:1–19:7	Acts 9:32–10:16	Ps. 104:1–9
☐ Day 184	2 Kings 19:8–20:21	Acts 10:17–33	Ps. 104:10–23
☐ Day 185	2 Kings 21:1–22:20	Acts 10:34–11:18	Ps. 104: 24–30
☐ Day 186	2 Kings 23	Acts 11:19–12:1	Ps. 104:31–35
☐ Day 187	2 Kings 24–25	Acts 12:18–13:13	Ps. 105:1–7
☐ Day 188	1 Chron. 1–2	Acts 13:14–43	Ps. 105:8–15
☐ Day 189	1 Chron. 3:1–5:10	Acts 13:44–14:10	Ps. 105:16–28
☐ Day 190	1 Chron. 5:11–6:81	Acts 14:11–28	Ps. 105:29–36
☐ Day 191	1 Chron. 7:1–9:9	Acts 15:1–18	Ps. 105:37–45
☐ Day 192	1 Chron. 9:10–11:9	Acts 15:19–41	Ps. 106:1–12

☐ Day 193	1 Chron. 11:10–12:40	Acts 16:1–15	Ps. 106:13–27
☐ Day 194	1 Chron. 13–15	Acts 16:16–40	Ps. 106:28–33
☐ Day 195	1 Chron. 16–17	Acts 17:1–14	Ps. 106:34–43
☐ Day 196	1 Chron. 18–20	Acts 17:15–34	Ps. 106:44–48
☐ Day 197	1 Chron. 21–22	Acts 18:1–23	Ps. 107:1–9
☐ Day 198	1 Chron. 23–25	Acts 18:24–19:10	Ps. 107:10–16
☐ Day 199	1 Chron. 26–27	Acts 19:11–22	Ps. 107:17–32
☐ Day 200	1 Chron. 28–29	Acts 19:23–41	Ps. 107:33–38
☐ Day 201	2 Chron. 1–3	Acts 20:1–16	Ps. 107:39–43
☐ Day 202	2 Chron. 4:1–6:11	Acts 20:17–38	Ps. 108
☐ Day 203	2 Chron. 6:12–7:10	Acts 21:1–14	Ps. 109:1–20
☐ Day 204	2 Chron. 7:11–9:28	Acts 21:15–32	Ps. 109:21–31
☐ Day 205	2 Chron. 9:29–12:16	Acts 21:33–22:16	Ps. 110:1–3
☐ Day 206	2 Chron. 13–15	Acts 22:17–23:11	Ps. 110:4–7
☐ Day 207	2 Chron. 16–17	Acts 23:12–24:21	Ps. 111
☐ Day 208	2 Chron. 18–19	Acts 24:22–25:12	Ps. 112
☐ Day 209	2 Chron. 20–21	Acts 25:13–27	Ps. 113
☐ Day 210	2 Chron. 22–23	Acts 26	Ps. 114
☐ Day 211	2 Chron. 24:1–25:16	Acts 27:1–20	Ps. 115:1–10
☐ Day 212	2 Chron. 25:17–27:9	Acts 27:21–28:6	Ps. 115:11–18
☐ Day 213	2 Chron. 28:1–29:19	Acts 28:7–31	Ps. 116:1–5
☐ Day 214	2 Chron. 29:20–30:27	Rom. 1:1–17	Ps. 116:6–19
☐ Day 215	2 Chron. 31–32	Rom. 1:18–32	Ps. 117
☐ Day 216	2 Chron. 33:1–34:7	Rom. 2	Ps. 118:1–18

☐ Day 217	2 Chron. 34:8–35:19	Rom. 3:1–26	Ps. 118:19–23
☐ Day 218	2 Chron. 35:20–36:23	Rom. 3:27–4:25	Ps. 118:24–29
☐ Day 219	Ezra 1–3	Rom. 5	Ps. 119:1–8
☐ Day 220	Ezra 4–5	Rom. 6:1–7:6	Ps. 119:9–16
☐ Day 221	Ezra 6:1–7:26	Rom. 7:7–25	Ps. 119:17–32
☐ Day 222	Ezra 7:27–9:4	Rom. 8:1–27	Ps. 119:33–40
☐ Day 223	Ezra 9:5–10:44	Rom. 8:28–39	Ps. 119:41–64
☐ Day 224	Neh. 1:1–3:16	Rom. 9:1–18	Ps. 119:65–72
☐ Day 225	Neh. 3:17–5:13	Rom. 9:19–33	Ps. 119:73–80
☐ Day 226	Neh. 5:14–7:73	Rom. 10:1–13	Ps. 119:81–88
☐ Day 227	Neh. 8:1–9:5	Rom. 10:14–11:24	Ps. 119:89–104
☐ Day 228	Neh. 9:6–10:27	Rom. 11:25–12:8	Ps. 119:105–120
☐ Day 229	Neh. 10:28–12:26	Rom. 12:9–13:7	Ps. 119:121–128
☐ Day 230	Neh. 12:27–13:31	Rom. 13:8–14:12	Ps. 119:129–136
☐ Day 231	Esther 1:1–2:18	Rom. 14:13–15:13	Ps. 119:137–152
☐ Day 232	Esther 2:19–5:14	Rom. 15:14–21	Ps. 119:153–168
☐ Day 233	Esther. 6–8	Rom. 15:22–33	Ps. 119:169–176
☐ Day 234	Esther 9–10	Rom. 16	Ps. 120–122
☐ Day 235	Job 1–3	1 Cor. 1:1–25	Ps. 123
☐ Day 236	Job 4–6	1 Cor. 1:26–2:16	Ps. 124–125
☐ Day 237	Job 7–9	1 Cor. 3	Ps. 126–127
☐ Day 238	Job 10–13	1 Cor. 4:1–13	Ps. 128–129
☐ Day 239	Job 14–16	1 Cor. 4:14–5:13	Ps. 130
☐ Day 240	Job 17–20	1 Cor. 6	Ps. 131

☐ Day 241	Job 21–23	1 Cor. 7:1–16	Ps. 132
☐ Day 242	Job 24–27	1 Cor. 7:17–40	Ps. 133–134
☐ Day 243	Job 28–30	1 Cor. 8	Ps. 135
☐ Day 244	Job 31–33	1 Cor. 9:1–18	Ps. 136:1–9
☐ Day 245	Job 34–36	1 Cor. 9:19–10:13	Ps. 136:10–26
☐ Day 246	Job 37–39	1 Cor. 10:14–11:1	Ps. 137
☐ Day 247	Job 40–42	1 Cor. 11:2–34	Ps. 138
☐ Day 248	Eccles. 1:1–3:15	1 Cor. 12:1–26	Ps. 139:1–6
☐ Day 249	Eccles. 3:16–6:12	1 Cor. 12:27–13:13	Ps. 139:7–18
☐ Day 250	Eccles. 7:1–9:12	1 Cor. 14:1–22	Ps. 139:19–24
☐ Day 251	Eccles. 9:13–12:14	1 Cor. 14:23–15:11	Ps. 140:1–8
☐ Day 252	SS 1–4	1 Cor. 15:12–34	Ps. 140:9–13
☐ Day 253	SS 5–8	1 Cor. 15:35–58	Ps. 141
☐ Day 254	Isa. 1–2	1 Cor. 16	Ps. 142
☐ Day 255	Isa. 3–5	2 Cor. 1:1–11	Ps. 143:1–6
☐ Day 256	Isa. 6–8	2 Cor. 1:12–2:4	Ps. 143:7–12
☐ Day 257	Isa. 9–10	2 Cor. 2:5–17	Ps. 144
☐ Day 258	Isa. 11–13	2 Cor. 3	Ps. 145
☐ Day 259	Isa. 14–16	2 Cor. 4	Ps. 146
☐ Day 260	Isa. 17–19	2 Cor. 5	Ps. 147:1–11
☐ Day 261	Isa. 20–23	2 Cor. 6	Ps. 147:12–20
☐ Day 262	Isa. 24:1–26:19	2 Cor. 7	Ps. 148
☐ Day 263	Isa. 26:20–28:29	2 Cor. 8	Ps. 149–150
☐ Day 264	Isa. 29–30	2 Cor. 9	Prov. 1:1–9

☐ Day 265	Isa. 31–33	2 Cor. 10	Prov. 1:10–22
☐ Day 266	Isa. 34–36	2 Cor. 11	Prov. 1:23–26
☐ Day 267	Isa. 37–38	2 Cor. 12:1–10	Prov. 1:27–33
☐ Day 268	Isa. 39–40	2 Cor. 12:11–13:14	Prov. 2:1–15
☐ Day 269	Isa. 41–42	Gal. 1	Prov. 2:16–22
☐ Day 270	Isa. 43:1–44:20	Gal. 2	Prov. 3:1–12
☐ Day 271	Isa. 44:21–46:13	Gal. 3:1–18	Prov. 3:13–26
☐ Day 272	Isa. 47:1–49:13	Gal 3:19–29	Prov. 3:27–35
☐ Day 273	Isa. 49:14–51:23	Gal 4:1–11	Prov. 4:1–19
☐ Day 274	Isa. 52–54	Gal. 4:12–31	Prov. 4:20–27
☐ Day 275	Isa. 55–57	Gal. 5	Prov. 5:1–14
☐ Day 276	Isa. 58–59	Gal. 6	Prov. 5:15–23
☐ Day 277	Isa. 60–62	Eph. 1	Prov. 6:1–5
☐ Day 278	Isa. 63:1–65:16	Eph. 2	Prov. 6:6–19
☐ Day 279	Isa. 65:17–66:24	Eph. 3:1–4:16	Prov. 6:20–26
☐ Day 280	Jer. 1–2	Eph. 4:17–32	Prov. 6:27–35
☐ Day 281	Jer. 3:1–4:22	Eph. 5	Prov. 7:1–5
☐ Day 282	Jer. 4:23–5:31	Eph. 6	Prov. 7:6–27
☐ Day 283	Jer. 6:1–7:26	Phil. 1:1–26	Prov. 8:1–11
☐ Day 284	Jer. 7:26–9:16	Phil. 1:27–2:18	Prov. 8:12–21
☐ Day 285	Jer. 9:17–11:17	Phil 2:19–30	Prov. 8:22–36
☐ Day 286	Jer. 11:18–13:27	Phil. 3	Prov. 9:1–6
☐ Day 287	Jer. 14–15	Phil. 4	Prov. 9:7–18
☐ Day 288	Jer. 16–17	Col. 1:1–23	Prov. 10:1–5

☐ Day 289	Jer. 18:1–20:6	Col. 1:24–2:15	Prov. 10:6–14
☐ Day 290	Jer. 20:7–22:19	Col. 2:16–3:4	Prov. 10:15–26
☐ Day 291	Jer. 22:20–23:40	Col. 3:5–4:1	Prov. 10:27–32
☐ Day 292	Jer. 24–25	Col. 4:2–18	Prov. 11:1–11
☐ Day 293	Jer. 26–27	1 Thes. 1:1–2:8	Prov. 11:12–21
☐ Day 294	Jer. 28–29	1 Thes. 2:9–3:13	Prov. 11:22–26
☐ Day 295	Jer. 30:1–31:22	1 Thes. 4:1–5:11	Prov. 11:27–31
☐ Day 296	Jer. 31:23–32:35	1 Thes. 5:12–28	Prov. 12:1–14
☐ Day 297	Jer. 32:36–34:7	2 Thes. 1–2	Prov. 12:15–20
☐ Day 298	Jer. 34:8–36:10	2 Thes. 3	Prov. 12:21–28
☐ Day 299	Jer. 36:11–38:13	1 Tim. 1:1–17	Prov. 13:1–4
☐ Day 300	Jer. 38:14–40:6	1 Tim. 1:18–3:13	Prov. 13:5–13
☐ Day 301	Jer. 40:7–42:22	1 Tim. 3:14–4:10	Prov. 13:14–21
☐ Day 302	Jer. 43–44	1 Tim. 4:11–5:16	Prov. 13:22–25
☐ Day 303	Jer. 45–47	1 Tim. 5:17–6:21	Prov. 14:1–6
☐ Day 304	Jer. 48:1–49:6	2 Tim. 1	Prov. 14:7–22
☐ Day 305	Jer. 49:7–50:16	2 Tim. 2	Prov. 14:23–27
☐ Day 306	Jer. 50:17–51:14	2 Tim. 3	Prov. 14:28–35
☐ Day 307	Jer. 51:15–64	2 Tim. 4	Prov. 15:1–9
☐ Day 308	Jer. 52–Lam. 1	Tit. 1:1–9	Prov. 15:10–17
☐ Day 309	Lam. 2:1–3:38	Tit. 1:10–2:15	Prov. 15:18–26
☐ Day 310	Lam. 3:39–5:22	Tit. 3	Prov. 15:27–33
☐ Day 311	Ezek. 1:1–3:21	Philemon 1	Prov. 16:1–9
☐ Day 312	Ezek. 3:22–5:17	Heb. 1:1–2:4	Prov. 16:10–21

☐ Day 313	Ezek. 6–7	Heb. 2:5–18	Prov. 16:22–33
☐ Day 314	Ezek. 8–10	Heb. 3:1–4:3	Prov. 17:1–5
☐ Day 315	Ezek. 11–12	Heb. 4:4–5:10	Prov. 17:6–12
☐ Day 316	Ezek. 13–14	Heb. 5:11–6:20	Prov. 17:13–22
☐ Day 317	Ezek. 15:1–16:43	Heb. 7:1–28	Prov. 17:23–28
☐ Day 318	Ezek. 16:44–17:24	Heb. 8:1–9:10	Prov. 18:1–7
☐ Day 319	Ezek. 18–19	Heb. 9:11–28	Prov. 18:8–17
☐ Day 320	Ezek. 20	Heb. 10:1–25	Prov. 18:18–24
☐ Day 321	Ezek. 21–22	Heb. 10:26–39	Prov. 19:1–8
☐ Day 322	Ezek. 23	Heb. 11:1–31	Prov. 19:9–14
☐ Day 323	Ezek. 24–26	Heb. 11:32–40	Prov. 19:15–21
☐ Day 324	Ezek. 27–28	Heb. 12:1–13	Prov. 19:22–29
☐ Day 325	Ezek. 29–30	Heb. 12:14–29	Prov. 20:1–18
☐ Day 326	Ezek. 31–32	Heb. 13	Prov. 20:19–24
☐ Day 327	Ezek. 33:1–34:10	Jas. 1	Prov. 20:25–3
☐ Day 328	Ezek. 34:11–36:15	Jas. 2	Prov. 21:1–8
☐ Day 329	Ezek. 36:16–37:28	Jas. 3	Prov. 21:9–18
☐ Day 330	Ezek. 38–39	Jas. 4:1–5:6	Prov. 21:19–24
☐ Day 331	Ezek. 40	Jas. 5:7–20	Prov. 21:25–31
☐ Day 332	Ezek. 41:1–43:12	1 Pet. 1:1–12	Prov. 22:1–9
☐ Day 333	Ezek. 43:13–44:31	1 Pet. 1:13–2:3	Prov. 22:10–23
☐ Day 334	Ezek. 45–46	1 Pet. 2:4–17	Prov. 22:24–29
☐ Day 335	Ezek. 47–48	1 Pet. 2:18–3:7	Prov. 23:1–9
☐ Day 336	Dan. 1:1–2:23	1 Pet. 3:8–4:19	Prov. 23:10–16

☐ Day 337	Dan. 2:24–3:30	1 Pet. 5	Prov. 23:17–25
☐ Day 338	Dan. 4	2 Pet. 1	Prov. 23:26–35
☐ Day 339	Dan. 5	2 Pet. 2	Prov. 24:1–18
☐ Day 340	Dan. 6:1–7:14	2 Pet. 3	Prov. 24:19–27
☐ Day 341	Dan. 7:15–8:27	1 John 1:1–2:17	Prov. 24:28–34
☐ Day 342	Dan. 9–10	1 John 2:18–29	Prov. 25:1–12
☐ Day 343	Dan. 11–12	1 John 3:1–12	Prov. 25:13–17
☐ Day 344	Hos. 1–3	1 John 3:13–4:16	Prov. 25:18–28
☐ Day 345	Hos. 4–6	1 John 4:17–5:21	Prov. 26:1–16
☐ Day 346	Hos. 7–10	2 John	Prov. 26:17–21
☐ Day 347	Hos. 11–14	3 John	Prov. 26:22–27:9
☐ Day 348	Joel 1:1–2:17	Jude	Prov. 27:10–17
☐ Day 349	Joel 2:18–3:21	Rev. 1:1–2:11	Prov. 27:18–27
☐ Day 350	Amos 1:1–4:5	Rev. 2:12–29	Prov. 28:1–8
☐ Day 351	Amos 4:6–6:14	Rev. 3	Prov. 28:9–16
☐ Day 352	Amos 7–9	Rev. 4:1–5:5	Prov. 28:17–24
☐ Day 353	Obad-Jonah	Rev. 5:6–14	Prov. 28:25–28
☐ Day 354	Mic. 1:1–4:5	Rev. 6:1–7:8	Prov. 29:1–8
☐ Day 355	Mic. 4:6–7:20	Rev. 7:9–8:13	Prov. 29:9–14
☐ Day 356	Nah. 1–3	Rev. 9–10	Prov. 29:15–23
☐ Day 357	Hab. 1–3	Rev. 11	Prov. 29:24–27
☐ Day 358	Zeph. 1–3	Rev. 12	Prov. 30:1–6
☐ Day 359	Hag. 1–2	Rev. 13:1–14:13	Prov. 30:7–16
☐ Day 360	Zech. 1–4	Rev. 14:14–16:3	Prov. 30:17–20

NOTES

NOTES

NOTES

NOTES

NOTES

NOTES

NOTES

NOTES

NOTES